family fare

AND OTHER RECIPES FROM THE **f** WORD

GORDON RAMSAY'S

family fare

AND OTHER RECIPES FROM THE f WORD

with Mark Sargeant
and Emily Quah

KEY PORTER BOOKS

photographs by Jill Mead

NOTES

Recipes give both standard American measures and metric measures. The two sets of measurements are not exact equivalents, so use one or the other, not a combination.

All herbs are fresh, and all pepper is freshly ground black pepper unless otherwise suggested.

Egg sizes are specified where they are critical, otherwise use large eggs. I recommend eggs from cage-free birds. If you are pregnant or in a vulnerable health group, avoid recipes containing raw egg whites or lightly cooked eggs.

My oven timings are for fan-assisted ovens. If you are using a conventional oven increase the temperature by 25°F (10°C). Individual ovens can deviate by as much as 10°C from the setting, either way. Get to know your oven and use an oven thermometer to check its accuracy. My timings are provided as guidelines, with a description of color or texture where appropriate.

CONTENTS

3138310402416

RECIPE LIST

INTRODUCTION

I was shocked to discover how many families never sit down to eat together. You don't necessarily have to be a big family in order to share food around a table and enjoy each other's company. And it doesn't have to be a Sunday, it can be a Saturday, it can be a Friday, any time of any day when families and friends can bond, sharing laughter as well as sadness. It's also an opportunity for individuals, especially children, to gain in confidence. The spine of my campaign is to reignite and reintroduce that special time of the week.

When I was growing up in Stratford-upon-Avon, we always had a family meal on Sunday. It didn't matter what else was happening, we always had a family meal. Invariably, it was a big main meal followed by the most amazing apple pie, or something like a trifle. And no one was allowed to leave the table until everyone had finished.

No matter how busy our current lifestyles are, or what is going on outside, family meals are really important. At home, Tana and I make sure we eat together as a family at least three times a week—usually Friday, Saturday, and, of course, on Sunday. Saturday lunches are always very casual. Sunday lunch has forever been routine. Even when the children were tiny and eating pureés, we still ate together. Like many other families with young children, we tend to rotate roast chicken, lamb, beef etc., introducing new flavors and different vegetables each week. As tastes broaden, so do the meals we share together.

The most exciting thing about this book is the way it is presented, with the recipes arranged as menus. Of course, these are entirely flexible—you can skip the appetizer if you like, or mix and match appetizers and desserts with main courses. But the menus take the effort out of planning a balanced three-course meal and they guide you on scheduling your time to ensure a stress-free meal.

I am determined to revive the family meal tradition, to take the intimidation out of cooking and get families back around the table. Join me and help to make my campaign work.

01 Mediterranean flavors

Sweet, succulent lamb in a fragrant herb coating with rustic vegetables and a dessert with a French twist to follow... divine. I love the scallop appetizer too, but for an easy option you could simply hand around bowls of little Niçoise olives and toast fingers spread with tapenade. This menu serves 4.

Pan-roasted scallops with cauliflower purée
Herb-crusted rack of lamb
+ Potatoes boulangère
+ Zucchini provençale

Baguette & butter pudding

planning your menu

A FEW DAYS AHEAD...
• Order the rack of lamb from your butcher and the scallops from the fish supplier (arranging to collect a day ahead, or get the shellfish on the day if possible).

SEVERAL HOURS IN ADVANCE...
• Make the baguette & butter pudding and let soak, ready to apply the sugar topping and cook later.
• For the appetizer, clean scallops and chill. Prepare caper dressing and vinaigrette.
• Make the herb crust for the lamb; score the meat, and return to the refrigerator.
• Prepare the potatoes boulangère and set aside, ready to cook.

TWO HOURS AHEAD...
• Bring the meat to room temperature.
• Prepare the ingredients for the zucchini provençale, ready to cook.
• Make the cauliflower purée for the appetizer and set aside.

ABOUT 30 MINUTES AHEAD...
• Take the scallops out of the refrigerator.
• Bake the potatoes boulangère.
• Sear the lamb, apply the herb crust, and finish cooking in the oven.
• Bake the pudding (in a second oven if you have one, or on a low oven shelf below the lamb while it is cooking).

JUST BEFORE SERVING...
• Warm the cauliflower purée through, pan-fry the scallops, and assemble the appetizer.
• Rest the meat while you eat the appetizer.
• Cook the zucchini provençale, carve the lamb, and serve with the potatoes.
• Let the pudding rest while you eat the main course.

10

PAN-ROASTED SCALLOPS WITH CAULIFLOWER PURÉE

66 This is a great appetizer that we keep coming back to, because the combination of flavors is truly outstanding. Sweet scallops served on a creamy cauliflower purée and topped with a sweet-and-salty caper dressing... simply divine. 99

4 servings

½ cup (100g) golden raisins
scant 1 cup (100g) capers in brine, rinsed
  and drained
12–16 large scallops, shelled and
  cleaned
1 tsp mild curry powder
sea salt and freshly ground black pepper
olive oil, for cooking

VINAIGRETTE:
1 tbsp sherry vinegar
3 tbsp olive oil

CAULIFLOWER PURÉE:
½ head of cauliflower, about ¾lb (350g),
  trimmed
2 tbsp (30g) butter
1–2 tbsp milk
⅓ cup (100ml) light cream

TIP To ensure that the scallops are cooked evenly, place them in a ring in the pan, arranging them in a clockwise order. A minute later, turn them over starting with the first scallop at the 12 o'clock position. This way, all the scallops should be cooked evenly.

Put the golden raisins, capers, and
⅓ cup (100ml) water into a small pan and bring to a boil. Tip into a food processor and whiz to a purée. For a smoother result, pass the mixture through a fine strainer.

For the vinaigrette, whisk the sherry vinegar
and olive oil together to emulsify and season with salt and pepper to taste. Set aside.

For the purée, cut the cauliflower into florets. Melt
the butter in a pan, add the cauliflower florets, and sauté for about 3 to 4 minutes. Add a little milk, cover, and sweat for 2 to 3 minutes, then pour in the cream and return to a gentle boil. Partially cover and cook for a few more minutes until the florets are soft. Season well.

Tip the cauliflower and cream into a food
processor and blend for a few minutes until smooth, scraping down the sides of the processor a few times. (It is much easier to do this while the mixture is still hot.)

Lightly sprinkle both sides of the scallops with
the curry powder and seasoning. Heat a little olive oil in a large nonstick skillet. Add the scallops and cook for just a minute on each side, turning them in the order they were put in. They should be nicely brown on both sides and feel springy when pressed. Remove from the pan to a warm plate and let rest for a minute.

Slice each scallop in half horizontally and
season well. Put 6–7 little spoonfuls of the cauliflower purée on each plate and top each with a scallop half. Drizzle with the caper dressing and vinaigrette and serve immediately.

13

HERB-CRUSTED RACK OF LAMB

❝ At the restaurant, our racks of lamb arrive French trimmed and ready to go. These are relatively small. Your local butcher may supply you with larger racks, which have more meat and fat extending to the top of the bones. Trim off the excess fat but don't waste the extra meat. You will need to cook these racks for an extra 5 to 10 minutes. ❞

4 servings

2 racks of lamb, cut in half
 (3–4 bones in each portion)
olive oil, for cooking
sea salt and freshly ground black pepper
2 tbsp English mustard

HERB CRUST:
4 slices of day-old bread, crusts removed
large handful of parsley
small handful of cilantro
small bunch of thyme
few rosemary sprigs
2oz (50g) Parmesan, freshly grated

Heat the oven to 400°F (200°C). Score the lamb fat in a criss-cross pattern and season well. Seal the racks in a hot ovenproof pan with a little olive oil until golden brown, about 4 minutes each side. Transfer the pan to the oven for 10 to 15 minutes to finish cooking the lamb. It should feel springy when pressed. Let rest while you prepare the herb crust.

Tear the bread into pieces and put into a food processor. Roughly chop the herb leaves and add to the processor with the Parmesan and a little seasoning. Whiz to fine crumbs, which will take on a bright green color. Brush the lamb with mustard and coat with the herb crust, patting it on firmly. Return the lamb to the pan and warm through in the oven for 5 minutes.

Slice the lamb into individual chops and serve three per person, with the Pommes boulangère and Zucchini provençale.

Pommes boulangère

Heat the oven to 400°F (200°C). Bring the stock to a boil with the thyme, rosemary, and 3 smashed garlic cloves added. Turn off the heat and let infuse for 20 minutes, then strain. Mince the other garlic cloves. Sauté the onions and chopped garlic in a little olive oil until softened, about 6 to 8 minutes. Meanwhile, peel the potatoes and finely slice, using a mandolin if possible.

Layer the potatoes and onions in a large shallow ovenproof dish, seasoning well as you do so and finishing with a layer of potatoes. Pour in enough stock to comes two-thirds up the side of the dish (you may not need all of it). Press down on the potatoes and finally drizzle a little olive oil on top. Bake for 35 to 40 minutes until golden brown on top and the potatoes are tender when pierced.

4 servings

1¾ cups (400ml) chicken stock
 (see page 246)
1 thyme sprig
2 rosemary sprigs
5 garlic cloves, peeled
2 large onions, peeled and sliced
a little olive oil, for cooking
4 large waxy potatoes, such as
 round red
sea salt and freshly ground
 black pepper

Zucchini provençale

servings

1 large zucchini

olive oil, for cooking

rosemary sprig, leaves minced

sea salt and freshly ground black pepper

tbsp balsamic vinegar

oz (175g) cherry tomatoes, halved

w basil sprigs, leaves torn

Cut the zucchini on the diagonal into ½ inch (1cm) thick slices. Heat a little olive oil in a large sauté pan. Add the zucchini with the chopped rosemary and sauté for a minute, seasoning well and adding a dash of balsamic vinegar. Tip in the cherry tomatoes and cook for 2 to 3 minutes, adding a little more olive oil, seasoning, and vinegar. Allow to cook until the zucchini and tomatoes have just begun to soften. Toss in the basil leaves, check the seasoning, and serve immediately.

BAGUETTE & BUTTER PUDDING

" This dessert has become a firm favorite on our restaurant menus. The thin pillowy texture of the baguette is perfect for soaking up the creamy custard, which is flavored with Cointreau though you can, of course, try different liqueurs. "

4–6 servings

4 tbsp (50g) unsalted butter, softened
4 tbsp apricot conserve
1 large French baguette, about 7oz (200g), thinly sliced
⅓ cup (60g) golden raisins or dried cranberries (or a mixture of both)
2 large eggs
2 large egg yolks
scant ¼ cup (40g) superfine sugar
1¼ cups (300ml) heavy cream
1¼ cups (300ml) milk
4 tbsp Cointreau, or more to taste
raw brown sugar, to sprinkle

TO SERVE:
½ cup (120ml) pouring cream
a little Cointreau (optional)

TIP This dessert is cooked in a bain-marie (water bath) to temper the oven heat. This prevents the custard from overheating, which can result in curdling.

Use a large piece
of the butter to grease the sides of a 6⅓-cup (1.5-liter) shallow ovenproof dish. Spread 1 tbsp of the conserve in the bottom of the dish. Butter the bread slices and arrange them in the dish in overlapping layers, sprinkling the dried fruit between.

Beat the eggs,
egg yolks, and superfine sugar together in a large bowl until creamy, then beat in the cream, milk, and Cointreau. Slowly pour this mixture over the bread. Press the bread slices down gently with your fingers so they are completely submerged. Let stand for about 20 minutes to allow the bread to soak up the custard. Preheat the oven to 350°F (180°C).

Stand the dish
in a roasting pan and surround with boiling water to come halfway up the sides of the dish. Sprinkle the raw brown sugar evenly over the top of the pudding and bake in the oven for 40 to 50 minutes until golden.

As soon as the dessert
is ready, warm the remaining apricot jam with 1 tbsp water until runny. Dab this glaze over the surface of the dessert with a pastry brush and let stand for 15 minutes before serving. The custard will continue to cook and firm up during this time. Serve warm with a drizzle of cream, flavored with a little Cointreau if you like.

02 Spring greens

Fresh spring flavors sing out from this colorful menu. Gooseberry sauce and spring greens are the perfect foil for rich duck breasts and the prepare-ahead dessert is truly refreshing. Vary the topping for the little tarts, making them as simple as you like. This menu serves 6.

Artichoke, asparagus, tomato & onion tart
Duck breast with spring greens & gooseberry sauce
Citrus dessert with passion fruit coulis

planning your menu

THE DAY BEFORE...
• Make the citrus dessert and the passion fruit coulis and refrigerate.

SEVERAL HOURS IN ADVANCE...
• For the appetizer, make the onion purée. Shape and bake the pastry bases.

AN HOUR IN ADVANCE...
• Prepare the spice mix, score the duck fat, and coat with the spice. Set aside at room temperature.
• For the tarts, blanch the asparagus, boil the quail's eggs, and prepare the other ingredients ready to assemble.
• Make the gooseberry sauce.
• Prepare the spring greens ready to cook.

JUST BEFORE SERVING...
• Assemble the appetizer.
• Pan-fry the duck breasts and put into the oven to finish cooking while you eat your appetizer.
• Rest the duck while you wilt the spring greens and reheat the sauce.
• Slice the duck and serve with the sauce.
• Turn out the dessert, slice, and serve with the coulis.

ARTICHOKE, ASPARAGUS, TOMATO & ONION TART

"My children call these gorgeous little tarts 'mini pizzas.' Indeed, you can adapt the toppings as you like. Semidried tomatoes are a good alternative to fresh ones and to save time, you could use ready-made tapenade in place of the onion purée."

6 servings

ONION PUREE:
olive oil, for cooking
6 onions, peeled and minced
sea salt and freshly ground black pepper
4 tbsp light cream

TART:
1lb 2oz (500g) ready-made puff pastry
flour, to dust
5oz (150g) asparagus tips
12 quail's eggs
5oz (150g) ready-cooked artichoke
   hearts, cut into wedges
5oz (150g) cherry tomatoes, halved
½ small red onion, peeled and finely
   sliced
small handful of chives, chopped
3–4 tbsp Classic vinaigrette
   (see page 247)
few arugula leaves, to garnish

TIP Lightly roll the boiled quail's eggs on the counter to gently crush the shells, making them easier to shell.

For the onion purée, heat a little olive oil in a pan, add the onions, and season well. Cover and cook over low heat, stirring occasionally, for 10 to 15 minutes until the onions are very soft. Meanwhile, heat the oven to 400°F (200°C).

Roll out the pastry thinly on a lightly floured surface and cut out 6 disks, using a 5–6-inch (13–15-cm) plate or saucer as a guide. Lay the pastry disks on a large baking sheet and prick all over with a skewer. Place another baking sheet on top of the pastry disks to weigh them down. Bake for 15 minutes until brown and crisp. Transfer to a wire rack to cool.

Add the cream to the onions and bring to a simmer. Tip the mixture into a blender or food processor and whiz to a fine paste. For a very smooth purée, push the onion paste through a strainer. Let cool.

Blanch the asparagus tips in a pan of boiling salted water for 2 minutes until tender. Remove with tongs and refresh in a bowl of iced water, then drain and tip into a large bowl.

Add the quail's eggs to the boiling water in the pan carefully, and cook for 2 minutes, 10 seconds. This will leave the eggs with runny yolks. Refresh under cold running water and peel off the shells.

Add the artichokes, tomatoes, red onion, and chives to the asparagus, drizzle with the vinaigrette, and toss to mix.

Spoon a little onion purée over the center of the pastry disks and pile the vegetables on top. Halve the quail's eggs and arrange on the vegetables. Scatter a few arugula leaves over, sprinkle with a little salt and pepper, and serve.

DUCK BREAST
WITH SPRING GREENS & GOOSEBERRY SAUCE

"Tart fruits such as gooseberries go really well with duck, because they cut through the richness of the meat. The spring greens add a touch of lightness to this meal."

6 servings

3 tbsp Szechwan peppercorns
sea salt and freshly ground black pepper
6 duck breasts with skin, about
   6oz (175g) each
1¼ cups (300ml) Sugar syrup
   (see page 248)
5oz (150g) gooseberries
⅔ cup (150ml) dry red wine
⅔ cup (150ml) brown Chicken (or duck)
   stock (see page 246)
3 tbsp gooseberry conserve or honey
few pieces of butter
14oz (400g) spring greens, cored and
   finely shredded

TIP If you prefer a smooth sauce, press the gooseberries through a fine strainer before adding them to the sauce.

Toast the peppercorns in a dry pan until fragrant, then tip into a mortar and pestle and add a little salt and pepper. Lightly crush the peppercorn mix. Score the skin of the duck breasts in a criss-cross pattern, then coat with the spice mixture.

Place the duck breasts, skin side down, in a dry ovenproof pan and cook over very low heat to render down most of the fat. This may take 10 to 15 minutes. Heat the oven to 400°F (200°C).

Heat the sugar syrup in a pan, meanwhile. Add the gooseberries and gently poach for 2 to 3 minutes. Let them cool in the sugar syrup.

For the sauce, boil the red wine in a pan for 7 to 8 minutes until reduced by half. Pour in the stock and again, reduce by half.

Turn up the heat under the duck breasts and fry until the skin is crisp. Turn them over and seal the other side for 1 to 2 minutes. Transfer the pan to the hot oven and cook for 8 to 10 minutes for medium-rare duck—it should be slightly springy when pressed.

In the meantime, stir the gooseberry conserve into the sauce and add a piece of butter for shine. Drain the gooseberries, add them to the sauce, and warm through. Taste and adjust the seasoning.

When ready, rest the duck on a warm plate for 10 minutes Wilt the spring greens with a couple of pieces of butter in a hot pan. Season well, then divide among warm serving plates. Thickly slice the duck breasts on the diagonal and fan out on top of the spring greens. Spoon the sauce over and around to serve.

CITRUS DESSERT WITH PASSION FRUIT COULIS

" This is a stunning dessert, worth the little extra time and patience required. It is also fat free, so perfect for anyone on a low-fat diet. You can set the dessert in a loaf pan or terrine and slice it to serve, or in individual molds. We use triangular molds in the restaurants, but you could use any shape. "

6–8 servings

2 pink grapefruit
2 white grapefruit
4 large seedless oranges
5 gelatin leaves
¾ cup (200ml) Sugar syrup
  (see page 248)

PASSION FRUIT COULIS:
2 ripe passion fruit
¾ cup (200ml) Sugar syrup
  (see page 248)

Slice off the tops and bottoms off the grapefruit and oranges, using a sharp, serrated knife, then cut away the remaining peel, removing the pith too. Segment the fruit by cutting the segments free from the membranes, holding the fruit over a strainer set on a bowl to catch the juice. Squeeze out the excess juice from the core of each fruit before discarding. Set aside the juice. Remove any membrane or pips left on the segments.

Lay the fruit segments on a tray lined with a clean dish towel and chill for an hour. This is to dry the fruit and prevent any excess juice from diluting the dessert as it sets.

Measure the citrus juice collected; you need ¾ cup (200ml). Soak the gelatin leaves in a bowl of cold water. Bring the sugar syrup to a boil in a pan, then remove from the heat. Squeeze out excess water from the gelatin leaves and add them to the hot syrup. Stir until the gelatin has dissolved, then mix with the citrus juice.

Arrange the grapefruit and orange segments randomly in a 2¼-lb (1-kg) loaf pan or terrine. Pour the gelatin mixture over the fruit segments and chill overnight until set.

For the coulis, simply halve the passion fruit and spoon the juice and seeds into the sugar syrup. Chill until needed.

To unmold the dessert, dip the pan in hot water for 2 seconds, then invert onto a board and give the pan a gentle shake to release the dessert. Cut into slices with a sharp knife and lift onto serving plates. Serve with a drizzle of passion fruit coulis.

25

"Family meals are the perfect excuse to get people together. It doesn't just have to be the immediate family—it can be friends, neighbors, relatives—remember Auntie Joan? Join me in getting family fare back on the menu."

03 Winter casserole

Slow-cooked beef in red wine followed by an all-time favorite dessert... this is comfort food at its best. An ideal family meal, especially if you're planning to go out in the morning, as the casserole tastes even better made a day ahead. This menu serves 6.

Celery & corn salad with blue cheese dressing

Beef casserole
+ Buttered savoy cabbage
+ Mustard mash

Knickerbocker glory

planning your menu

THE DAY BEFORE...
• Make the casserole and refrigerate overnight (or make it early on the day).
• Make the gelatin for the dessert and chill to set.

AN HOUR OR TWO AHEAD...
• Take the casserole out of the refrigerator to bring to room temperature.
• Peel the potatoes for the mash and immerse in cold water.
• Shred, blanch, and refresh the cabbage.
• Prepare the ingredients for the salad ready to assemble.

ABOUT 30 MINUTES IN ADVANCE...
• Reheat the casserole in a low oven.
• For the dessert, prepare the fruit, chop the gelatin, and crush the amaretti. Set aside, ready to assemble.
• Cook the potatoes and prepare the mash; keep warm.

JUST BEFORE SERVING...
• Assemble the appetizer and serve.
• Sauté the cabbage, then serve the main course.
• Assemble the knickerbocker glories just before serving.

CELERY & CORN SALAD WITH BLUE CHEESE DRESSING

" Comprising three simple ingredients, this is a wonderfully light, refreshing salad. Celery, corn salad and mild blue creamy cheese is one of my favorite combinations. I like to use a mild blue from the Loire and Puy-de-Dôme regions, called Fourme d'Ambert, which is regarded as one of the oldest of all French cheeses. It has a slightly sweet, nutty flavor and a lovely, creamy texture. You can also serve this salad as a light lunch, with plenty of warm, crusty bread. "

6 servings

5 celery stalks, trimmed
7oz (200g) corn salad
5oz (150g) mild blue creamy cheese
6 tbsp Classic vinaigrette (see page 247)
sea salt and freshly ground black pepper
handful of crushed, toasted walnuts
   (optional)

TIP If you can't buy Fourme d'Ambert from your local cheese store, then substitute Gorgonzola, Bleu d'Auvergne, or any mild, crumbly blue cheese.

Finely chop the celery and put it into a large salad bowl. Twist off any thick root ends from the corn salad, then add to the celery. Crumble half the cheese into the bowl, then drizzle with 3–4 tbsp of the vinaigrette and toss to mix.

Pile the salad onto individual plates, crumble over the remaining cheese, and sprinkle with salt and pepper. For added texture, scatter over a handful of crushed walnuts. Drizzle over the remaining vinaigrette and serve.

BEEF CASSEROLE

> ❝ This casserole is the perfect winter warmer. Braising beef is slowly cooked with herbs and vegetables in red wine, which gives the stew a depth of color and a wonderful rich flavor. Flavored mash and sautéed cabbage are ideal accompaniments. ❞

6 servings

1¾lb (800g) braising beef

3 tbsp all-purpose flour

sea salt and freshly ground black pepper

olive oil, for cooking

7oz (200g) smoked bacon, cut into small cubes

2 medium carrots, peeled

1 small celeriac, about 1lb 9oz (700g), peeled

5oz (150g) pearl onions (or baby shallots), peeled

few thyme sprigs

2 bay leaves

9oz (250g) crimini mushrooms, trimmed halved if large

1 tsp tomato paste

2 cups (500ml) red wine

1¼ cups (300ml) beef or brown Chicken stock (see page 246)

handful of Italian parsley, chopped

Heat the oven to 300°F (150°C).

Cut the beef into bite-size chunks. Season the flour with salt and pepper and toss the meat in the flour to coat. Heat a little olive oil in a large cast-iron casserole over medium heat. Sear the beef briefly in two or three batches until browned all over, then transfer to a plate and set aside.

Add the bacon to the casserole

and sauté gently until lightly golden, adding a little olive oil if necessary. Meanwhile, cut the carrots and celeriac into ¾-inch (2-cm) cubes. Tip them into the pan with the whole onions, thyme, and bay leaves and stir over medium heat for 5 minutes until the vegetables begin to soften. Stir in the mushrooms and tomato paste and sauté for another 2 to 3 minutes.

Pour in the red wine and scrape the bottom of

the pan with a wooden spoon to deglaze. Add the stock and bring the liquid to a boil, then lower the heat and simmer for a few minutes. Return the beef to the casserole and stir to immerse the meat in the liquid completely. Put the lid on the casserole and cook in the oven for 2½ hours or until the beef is very tender.

Check the seasoning, then scatter the

chopped parsley over the stew. Serve with the accompaniments.

Buttered savoy cabbage

Finely slice the cabbage and blanch in a pan of boiling salted water for 2 minutes. Drain, and if not serving immediately, refresh under cold running water. Drain well again. Just before serving, melt the butter in a wide, heavy pan, add the blanched cabbage, and season well with salt and pepper. Toss over medium heat for 1 to 2 minutes until the cabbage is just tender. Serve at once.

6 servings

1 savoy cabbage, trimmed
sea salt and freshly ground black
  pepper
2 tbsp (25g) unsalted butter

Mustard mash

servings

¼lb (1kg) mealy potatoes, such as
Russet
sea salt and freshly ground black pepper
cup (150ml) heavy cream
½ tbsp (85g) butter, cut into cubes
tbsp wholegrain mustard
-2 tbsp Dijon mustard

Peel the potatoes and cut into large, even-size chunks. Cook in boiling salted water for 12 to 15 minutes until tender. Drain well, then return to the pan and dry out for 1 to 2 minutes over medium heat. Mash the potatoes well, preferably using a potato ricer back into the pan. For a very smooth result, push the mashed potato through a fine strainer. Gently heat the cream and slowly stir into the mashed potato. Season well. Cook gently for 5 minutes, then gradually beat in the butter, a cube at a time. Finally stir in the mustards and season with salt and pepper to taste. Serve warm.

KNICKERBOCKER GLORY

" Admittedly a little 'over-the-top', this tempting dessert is an adult-version of a childhood treat. To accommodate children, cook the cherries in sugar syrup instead of kirsch. If you prefer, melt the chocolate buttons and pour the warm chocolate sauce over the ice cream, just before serving. Provide thin, long-handled serving spoons so everyone can delve down through the layers. "

6 servings

4³⁄₄oz (140g) package strawberry-
flavored gelatin
10oz (300g) ripe cherries, pitted
5 tbsp kirsch
¼ cup (50g) superfine sugar
1 small ripe mango
scant ¾ cup (100g) strawberries,
hulled
2 clementines
2 cups (500ml) good-quality vanilla
ice cream
2oz (50g) amaretti cookies
1½oz (40g) chocolate buttons

Break the gelatin into small pieces and put into a heatproof bowl. Pour on 3 tbsp boiling water and microwave on high for 1 to 1½ minutes. Stir until completely dissolved, then mix in 1¾ cups (400ml) cold water. Pour into a shallow bowl or loaf pan and chill overnight to set.

Place the cherries in a nonstick pan, sprinkle with the kirsch and sugar, and cook over high heat for 1 to 2 minutes until the cherries are soft but still holding their shape. Remove from the heat and let cool.

Put six tall glasses into the refrigerator to chill, ready for serving.

Peel the mango and cut the flesh away from the seed, then chop into ½-inch (1-cm) cubes. Quarter or slice the strawberries depending on size. Peel the clementines and slice them horizontally into thin circles.

Unmold the gelatin onto a board and roughly chop into small pieces. Lightly crush the amaretti cookies in a bowl with the end of a rolling pin.

To assemble, layer the cherries, mango, clementines, chopped gelatin, ice cream, strawberries, and chocolate buttons in the chilled glasses. Top with a final scoop of ice cream and sprinkle with the crushed amaretti cookies. Serve immediately.

5 ways with...CABBAGE

Savoy cabbage with marjoram
Serves 4–6

Trim and finely shred 1 small savoy cabbage. Blanch in a pan of boiling salted water for 2 to 3 minutes until tender; drain well. Melt 4 tbsp butter in a wide heavy pan. Toss in the cabbage and season well. Add the chopped leaves from a few marjoram sprigs, fold through, and serve warm. Lovely with chicken or fish dishes.

Bubble & squeak
Serves 4

Trim and finely shred ½ savoy cabbage. Blanch in a pan of boiling salted water for 2 to 3 minutes until tender; drain well. Mix the blanched cabbage with 1¼lb (500g) cooked mashed potatoes and season generously with salt and pepper. With lightly floured hands, shape the potato and cabbage mixture into individual patties. Heat 2 tbsp butter and 2 tbsp olive oil in a heavy skillet and cook the patties over low heat for several minutes until a crust forms on the bottom. Turn over and cook the other side until golden brown and crisp. Serve warm with Sunday lunch roasts.

Brussels sprouts gratinée
Serves 6

Cook 1¾lb (750g) trimmed Brussels sprouts in boiling salted water for 6 to 8 minutes until just tender. Drain and refresh under cold running water, then cut in half. Melt 1½ tbsp butter in a pan and stir in 2 tbsp all-purpose flour. Cook, stirring, for 1 to 2 minutes over low heat. Add a pinch of dry English mustard, a pinch of cayenne, and salt and pepper. Gradually whisk in 1¼ cups (300ml) milk, a little at a time, to make a smooth sauce. Let simmer, stirring frequently, until the sauce thickens and coats the back of a wooden spoon. Over very low heat, stir in ¾ cup (70g) grated sharp Cheddar until melted. When ready to serve, toss the Brussels sprouts with the sauce, place in a large gratin dish (or two smaller ones) and sprinkle with some more grated cheese. Place under a hot broiler for a few minutes until the topping is golden brown, then serve. A good accompaniment to roast chicken or a fish pie.

Braised red cabbage
Serves 4–6

Heat the oven to 350°F (180°C). Quarter, core, and finely shred 1 red cabbage and place in a large ovenproof casserole with ¾ cup (200ml) clear malt vinegar, ¾ cup (150g) brown sugar, and ⅔ cup (150g) melted unsalted butter. Season generously with salt and pepper and stir well. Cook in the oven for 1½ to 1¾ hours, stirring every 30 minutes to prevent the top from drying out. If there is still a fair amount of liquid, strain it off and boil until reduced to a syrupy sauce, then pour back over the cabbage and toss to coat. Superb with game birds, such as wild pigeon, squab, or duck.

Red cabbage slaw
Serves 6

Quarter, core, and finely shred 1 red cabbage and place in a large salad bowl. Grate 2 peeled carrots and 2 peeled, cored crisp apples (such as Granny Smiths) and add them to the cabbage with a squeeze of lemon juice, ½ cup toasted walnut pieces and 3 tbsp golden raisins. Toss well to mix.

For the dressing, beat together ½ cup (120ml) Mayonnaise (see page 247), 4 tbsp strained plain yogurt, and 1 tbsp orange juice in a bowl. Season with salt and pepper to taste and stir in 2 tbsp chopped chives. Spoon the dressing over the salad and toss until well coated. Cover and chill for about half an hour. Toss the salad again just before serving. Ideal with a barbecue or *alfresco* meal.

04 Chicken chic

I love the subtle flavors running through this menu—a velvety soup of white beans, a mushroom-infused sauce to enhance chicken, and a comforting apple sponge to finish. For a lighter dessert, you could omit the sponge and simply serve the caramelized apples with crème anglaise. This menu serves 4.

Haricot soup with jumbo shrimp

Chicken breast with a morel velouté

+ Pommes purée

+ Asparagus with herb butter

Gordon's apple pudding

planning your menu

THE DAY BEFORE...
• For the soup, cook the haricot beans, purée, and refrigerate.
• Prepare the chicken crowns and chill.
• Make the herb butter for the asparagus and chill.

SEVERAL HOURS IN ADVANCE...
• Take the chicken (and the butter and eggs for the dessert) out of the refrigerator.
• Make the morel velouté.
• Soak the golden raisins and caramelize the apples for the dessert. Let cool.

TWO HOURS AHEAD...
• Make the pommes purée.
• Blanch the shrimp for the soup.
• Prepare the flavored crème fraîche and refrigerate.
• Poach the chicken crowns and let rest; don't chill.

FROM AN HOUR AHEAD...
• Carve out the chicken breasts.
• Make and bake the apple pudding.
• Prepare the asparagus ready for cooking.

JUST BEFORE SERVING...
• Reheat the bean purée and make the soup (ready to whisk in the butter at the last minute). Sauté the shrimp.
• Pan-fry the chicken breasts and reheat the velouté.
• Finish the soup and rest the chicken while you have the appetizer.
• Reheat the pommes purée adding a few extra pieces of butter, cook the asparagus, and serve the main course.
• Leave the pudding at room temperature to cool slightly while you eat the main course, then serve with the crème fraîche.

HARICOT SOUP WITH JUMBO SHRIMP

" Puréed haricot beans provide a velvety background to jumbo shrimp—a concept we call *terre et mer*, which combines the flavors of the land and sea. In a dish like this, we generally use chicken stock as the base for the soup, as fish stock would overpower the distinctive but delicate flavor of the beans. "

4 servings

1⅓ cups (250g) dried haricot beans, soaked overnight
1 small onion, peeled and halved
1 carrot, peeled and halved
1 bouquet garni (thyme, bay leaf, and parsley tied together)
3⅓ cups (800ml) Court bouillon (see page 247)
18 jumbo shrimp, shelled and deveined
1¼ cups (300ml) Chicken (or vegetable) stock (see page 246)
⅔ cup (150ml) heavy cream
sea salt and freshly ground black pepper
2 tbsp (30g) cold butter, cut into cubes, plus a few pieces for cooking
handful of chives, minced
olive oil, to drizzle

Drain the haricot beans and place in a pan. Add the onion, carrot, and bouquet garni and cover with cold water. Bring to a boil and boil steadily for 10 minutes, then lower the heat to a simmer. Partially cover the pan and cook for 1½ to 2 hours until the beans are soft, stirring occasionally and topping off with boiling water if they appear dry. Drain the beans and discard the onion, carrot, and bouquet garni. Scoop out about 4 tbsp beans and set aside for the garnish.

Whiz the beans in a blender to a smooth purée, adding a touch of boiling water if necessary (to get the blades moving) and scraping down the sides a couple of times. For a really smooth soup, push the purée through a fine strainer.

Bring the court bouillon to a boil in a pan, add the shrimp, and blanch for 30 seconds, then drain and refresh under cold running water. Cut each shrimp into two or three bite-size pieces if you like.

Pour the bean purée into a pan and reheat gently, then whisk in the stock and cream and season with salt and pepper to taste. Whisk in the cold butter, a piece at a time, using a hand-held stick blender if you like—to froth up the soup.

Sauté the shrimp and reserved beans with a few pieces of butter to heat through. Season well, add the chives, and toss through. Pile into the center of warm bowls, pour the soup around them, and serve, drizzled with a little olive oil.

CHICKEN BREAST WITH A MOREL VELOUTÉ

66 This is the perfect way to cook chicken breasts—gently poach them on the bone to keep the meat flavorful and succulent, then pan-fry to give them a golden, crisp skin. Dried morels lend an intense flavor to the cream sauce. 99

4 servings

2 free-range chickens, about 2–2¼lb (900g–1kg) each
1 head of garlic (unpeeled), halved horizontally
sea salt and freshly ground black pepper
2 tbsp chicken bouillon powder
1 tbsp black peppercorns, lightly crushed
1 tbsp coriander seeds, lightly crushed
1 thyme sprig
2 bay leaves
2 leeks, trimmed and roughly chopped
2 carrots, peeled and roughly chopped
2 celery stalks, trimmed and roughly chopped
olive oil, for cooking
few pieces of butter

MOREL VELOUTÉ:
10–12 dried morels
olive oil, for cooking
3 large shallots, peeled and finely sliced
1 thyme sprig
1 garlic clove, peeled and crushed
¾ cup (175ml) dry white wine
1 cup (250ml) heavy cream

Remove the legs, wings, and pope's nose from the
chickens, to leave the crown of the birds. (Save the legs and wings for another dish.) Put the garlic in the cavities and season well. Soak the dried morels for the velouté in hot water for 20 minutes.

Two-thirds fill a large pan with cold water (enough to
cover the chickens). Add the bouillon powder, peppercorns, coriander seeds, herbs, and vegetables. Bring to a boil and simmer for 10 minutes. Add the chicken crowns and poach for 10 to 12 minutes or until the breasts feel firm. (Depending on the pan, you may need to poach them one at a time.) Remove from the pan and let rest for 5 minutes. Set aside the poaching stock.

Make the velouté in the meantime. Drain and chop
the morels, reserving the liquid. Heat a little olive oil in a pan and sauté the shallots, thyme, and garlic for 5 to 6 minutes until golden. Add the morels, a little more oil and seasoning. Cook for 5 to 6 minutes, then carefully pour in most of the morel soaking liquor (leaving the sediment behind). Add the wine and bubble until almost totally reduced. Add 2–3 ladlefuls of the reserved chicken poaching stock and boil for 8 to 10 minutes until reduced by half. Add the cream and simmer until thickened to the consistency of light cream. Pass the sauce through a strainer, pressing the mushrooms and shallots to extract as much flavor as possible. Season the sauce and return to the pan.

Carve out the breasts from the crowns carefully
and pat the skin dry with paper towels. Heat a little olive oil in a nonstick skillet and cook the chicken breasts until the skin is crisp and golden, 3 to 4 minutes each side. Add a few pieces of butter to the pan and spoon over the breasts during the final minute of cooking to keep them moist.

Rest the chicken while you reheat the velouté. Slice
each chicken breast in two horizontally and season each half. Arrange on warm plates, pour the sauce around, and serve with the accompaniments.

Pommes purée

Put the potatoes in a pan of cold water and bring to a boil.
Lower the heat and simmer for 15 to 20 minutes or until they feel tender when pierced with a knife. Drain and peel while still hot (wearing rubber gloves to protect your hands from the heat if you like). Push the potatoes through a ricer or mouli. For a smoother result, press the mashed potatoes through a fine strainer with a spatula. Meanwhile, heat the milk in a pan. Toss the puréed potatoes in a dry pan to dry out a little, then beat in the butter and season with salt and pepper. Just as the milk comes to a boil, pour onto the potatoes and beat well. (If you want a thinner purée, beat in a little boiling water.) Whisk in a few extra pieces of butter for a rich, silky finish.

4 servings

2¼lb (1kg) floury potatoes, such as Russet, well scrubbed
⅓ cup (100ml) milk
4 tbsp butter, plus a few pieces
sea salt and freshly ground black pepper

Asparagus with herb butter

4 servings

20 asparagus spears

HERB BUTTER:
¾ cup (185g) unsalted butter, softened
1 tsp minced tarragon
1 tsp minced Italian parsley
1 tsp minced chervil
sea salt and freshly ground black pepper

For the herb butter, beat the softened butter
with the chopped herbs, using a wooden spoon. Season well with salt and pepper. Spoon the herb butter onto a piece of plastic wrap, forming a sausage shape. Roll in the plastic wrap and wrap tightly, twisting the ends to seal. Chill until firm.

Trim the asparagus by snapping off the base of
the stalks. Bring a pan of salted water to a boil and blanch the asparagus for 3 to 4 minutes or until tender. Meanwhile, unwrap and thinly slice the herb butter. Drain the asparagus and serve each portion topped with a few slices of herb butter.

TIP Herb butter is a simple, effective way to dress up fish, shellfish, chicken, and vegetables. It can be frozen for up to a month, so make up a batch and use as required.

GORDON'S APPLE PUDDING

" This is my update on Eve's pudding, a homely baked apple pudding that's been around for ages. To enhance the flavor, I caramelize the apples with sugar and butter to give them a richness that is missing from simply stewed apples. My guests at the restaurant loved it, so I've made this generous enough for seconds! **"**

6 servings

¼ cup (50g) golden raisins
3 tbsp Calvados
1 cup (240g) unsalted butter, plus
   extra to grease
3 Braeburn or Pink Lady apples
scant 1 cup (175g) raw brown sugar
2 large eggs, beaten
generous 1 cup (150g) self-rising
   flour
finely grated zest of 1 lemon
2–3 tbsp milk
⅓ cup (30g) slivered almonds
   (optional)
confectioners' sugar, to dust
   (optional)

TO SERVE:
1 vanilla bean
¾ cup (200g) crème fraîche

Heat the oven
to 375°F (190°C). Soak the golden raisins in the Calvados. Lightly grease a 10-inch (25-cm) cake pan or an ovenproof dish.

Peel, core, and chop
the apples. Heat a nonstick skillet over medium heat, then add the apples with 1 tbsp (15g) butter and one-third of the sugar. Cook until they begin to caramelize, tossing them to ensure they color evenly. Tip in the golden raisins and Calvados and cook for another 5 to 10 minutes until the apples are tender. Transfer the apple mixture to the prepared pan, spread evenly, and let cool.

Meanwhile,
cream the remaining butter and sugar together. Beat in the eggs a little at a time, stirring in a spoonful of the flour if the mixture looks like it will split at any point. Fold in the flour and lemon zest, alternately with the milk. The mixture will be quite thick—add just enough milk to get the cake batter to a dropping consistency.

Pour the cake batter
over the apples and sprinkle with the slivered almonds and a dusting of confectioners' sugar if you like. Bake for about 30 to 35 minutes until the top is golden brown and a skewer inserted in the middle comes out clean. Run a thin knife around the edge of the pan and let cool slightly.

Split the vanilla bean
and scrape out the seeds with the back of a knife, adding them to the crème fraîche. Whip until evenly blended and creamy. Serve the pudding warm, with a generous dollop of vanilla crème fraîche.

05 Easy entertaining

Simple, elegant recipes are the key to stress-free entertaining and this menu features some of the best — an easy salad appetizer, pan-fried fish, and a delicate rice dessert, which can be made ahead. As an alternative appetizer, top chicory leaves with fresh pear slices, crumbled mild blue cheese, and a drizzle of vinaigrette. This menu serves 4.

Seared beef salad with sweet mustard dressing
Pan-fried sea bass with broccoli & sorrel sauce
Cardamom & rose water fragrant rice

planning your menu

A FEW DAYS AHEAD...
• Order the sea bass from the fish supplier (ask him to fillet it for you). Arrange to collect it on the day if possible, otherwise the day before.

THE DAY BEFORE...
• Make the fish velouté and keep chilled.

SEVERAL HOURS IN ADVANCE...
• Make the rice pudding and chill.
• For the appetizer, sear the beef and refrigerate. Make the dressing.

AN HOUR AHEAD...
• Check the fish fillets for any pin bones and bring to room temperature.
• Prepare the salad ingredients for the appetizer, ready to assemble.

JUST BEFORE SERVING...
• Stir the cream into the rice pudding and divide between glasses; chill.
• Toss the beef in the dressing with the herbs and plate the appetizer, then serve.
• Pan-fry the fish fillets, blanch the broccoli, and finish the sauce, then serve.
• Top the rice puddings with a spoonful of jam and serve.

SEARED BEEF SALAD
WITH SWEET MUSTARD DRESSING

" Inspired by steak tartare, this seared beef salad is perfect for those who are not accustomed to eating meat raw. Small cubes of beef are seared, chopped, and tossed with honey mustard dressing. The chicory acts as a refreshing palate cleanser between each bite. If making in advance, don't dress the beef until the last minute, because the vinegar in the dressing will 'cook' the beef and discolor the herbs. "

servings

live oil, for cooking and to drizzle
⅓lb (600g) beef tenderloin, cut into large 1½-inch (4-cm) chunks
ea salt and freshly ground black pepper
large red chicory bulb, trimmed
large white chicory bulb, trimmed
mall bunch of mint, leaves chopped
mall bunch of Italian parsley, leaves chopped

RESSING:
tbsp Dijon mustard
tbsp cider or white wine vinegar
tbsp runny honey
tbsp soy sauce
tbsp olive oil

Heat a large skillet until very hot and add a little olive oil. Season the beef with salt and pepper and sear for 3 to 4 minutes until browned on all sides. (You don't want to cook the beef chunks through, just sear them on the outside.) Let cool completely. If preparing in advance, tip into a bowl, drizzle with a little more olive oil, and refrigerate.

For the dressing, mix the ingredients together and season with salt and pepper to taste. Separate the chicory leaves.

Just before serving, cut the seared beef into small cubes. Place in a bowl and toss with the dressing and chopped herbs. Divide the beef among four serving plates, centering it using a pastry ring for a professional look if you like. Garnish the plate with chicory leaves (saving the larger outer leaves for another dish). Drizzle with a little olive oil, sprinkle with sea salt, and serve immediately.

PAN-FRIED SEA BASS WITH BROCCOLI & SORREL SAUCE

" Peppery sorrel adds freshness and a mild acidity that counters the richness of sea bass and the velouté in this recipe. You can usually find sorrel in farmers' markets during the summer—it's a shame that supermarkets don't stock it, as these leaves truly complement fish, veal, and poultry. "

4 servings

4 sea bass fillets, skin on, about 6oz
  (175g) each
olive oil, for cooking and to drizzle
sea salt and freshly ground black pepper
2 heads of broccoli, cut into florets
1¼ cups (300ml) fish Velouté
  (see page 247)
handful of sorrel leaves, shredded

Check the bass fillets for small pin bones, removing any with tweezers. Using a sharp knife, lightly score the skin at ½ inch (1cm) intervals. Heat a little olive oil in a large skillet until hot. Season the fish fillets and place them in the pan, skin side down. Cook, without moving, for 2 to 3 minutes until the skin is crisp and the fish is cooked two-thirds of the way through. Turn the fillets and cook the other side for about 30 seconds.

While the fish is cooking, blanch the broccoli in boiling salted water for 2 minutes and drain well. Drizzle with a little olive oil and season with salt and pepper. Keep warm.

Transfer the fish to a warm plate and lightly cover with a piece of foil. Pour the fish velouté into the pan and scrape up the sediment with a wooden spoon to deglaze the pan. Simmer for a few minutes, then add half of the shredded sorrel and take off the heat.

Divide the broccoli among warm serving plates and lay the sea bass fillets on top. Pour the sauce around the plate and garnish with the remaining shredded sorrel.

CARDAMOM & ROSE WATER FRAGRANT RICE

" Cardamom and rose water lend a perfumed, North African flavor to this delicate chilled rice pudding. I like to top it with a spoonful of quince jam, which complements the rose water and adds an extra touch of sweetness. If you can't find quince jam, use strawberry jam or serve the pudding on its own. "

4–6 servings

1¼ cups (300ml) heavy cream
8–10 cardamom pods, lightly crushed
½ cup (100g) superfine sugar
scant 1 cup (200g) pudding rice
pinch of fine sea salt
1 tsp rose water
4–6 tsp quince or strawberry jam

Pour the cream into a small pan, add the cardamom and sugar, and stir over gentle heat until the sugar has dissolved. Increase the heat and as soon as the cream begins to bubble, remove the pan from the heat and set aside to infuse for an hour. Don't worry if a skin forms on the surface, it will be strained out.

Put the rice into another pan with 1¾ cups (400ml) water and a pinch of salt. Give it a stir, bring to a boil, and then lower the heat to a simmer. Cover and cook for 15 to 20 minutes. Leaving the lid on, remove the pan from the heat and let stand for 5 minutes. Spread the rice out on a plate to cool completely.

Strain the cream through a fine strainer into a bowl, to remove the cardamom pods and seeds. Add the rose water, then stir two-thirds of the cream into the cooled rice. (Hold back some cream to loosen the rice before serving.) Cover the bowls of rice and remaining cream with plastic wrap and chill for at least 2 hours.

When ready to serve, stir the reserved cream into the chilled rice and spoon into individual glasses. Top each with a teaspoonful of quince jam.

NEARLY A QUARTER OF HOUSEHOLDS HAVEN'T COOKED USING FRESH INGREDIENTS IN THE PAST WEEK.

"Fresh means healthy. It's not rocket science."

if you share my passion for vibrant flavors that set the taste buds tingling, you'll love this menu. The garlicky mayonnaise is a great dip for shrimp or grilled veg, such as asparagus, zucchini, and peppers, if clams aren't to your taste. This menu serves 6–8.

Clams with aïoli

Roast rump of lamb with herb couscous
   + Spiced eggplant purée

Summary pudding

planning your menu

THE DAY BEFORE...
 • Make the summer pudding, weigh down, and chill overnight.
 • Put the lamb to marinate in the refrigerator.
 • Dégorge the eggplants, deep-fry, and let drain overnight.

AN HOUR OR TWO IN ADVANCE...
 • For the appetizer, clean the clams and make the aïoli.
 • Prepare the eggplant purée.

ABOUT 15 MINUTES AHEAD...
 • Pan-fry the lamb and put into the oven to finish cooking. Soak the couscous in boiling stock.

JUST BEFORE SERVING...
 • Cook the clams.
 • Add the vinaigrette and herbs to the couscous and fork through; keep warm.
 • Rest the meat while you eat the appetizer.
 • Reheat the eggplant purée, slice the lamb, and serve the main course.
 • Turn out the summer pudding and serve with cream.

CLAMS WITH AÏOLI

> *For me, these are as satisfying as moules marinière. The aïoli works perfectly with the clams, which should be just cooked—there's nothing worse than overcooked, rubbery shellfish. Take the pan off the heat as soon as the clams have opened up their shells. Serve with a nice, rustic ficelle or a crusty baguette.*

6–8 servings

- 4½–5½lb (2–2.5kg) fresh clams, cleaned
- 3–4 tbsp olive oil, plus extra to drizzle
- 3 banana shallots (or 6 medium shallots), peeled and thinly sliced
- few thyme sprigs
- 4 bay leaves
- splash of dry white wine
- small bunch of Italian parsley, leaves only chopped

AÏOLI:
- ⅓ cup (100ml) Mayonnaise (see page 247)
- 2 garlic cloves, peeled and finely crushed
- pinch of paprika
- sea salt and freshly ground black pepper

TIP To clean the clams, put them in a large bowl of cold water, leave for 5 minutes, then drain. Repeat twice more, replacing with fresh water each time. Discard any open clams.

First, make the aïoli. Mix the mayonnaise with the crushed garlic, paprika, and salt and pepper to taste until evenly combined. Set aside.

To cook the clams, you will need one very large or two smaller heavy pans. Heat the olive oil in the pan(s), add the shallots, and sauté for 3 to 4 minutes to soften. Tip in the clams, add the thyme and bay leaves with a splash of wine, and cover with a tight-fitting lid. Give the pan a good shake and let the clams steam for 4 to 5 minutes until the shells have opened. Take the pan off the heat.

Using a slotted spoon, transfer the clams to serving bowls, throwing away any that haven't opened.

Stir enough aïoli into the pan juices to thicken them (about 3–4 tbsp), then add the chopped parsley. Spoon the sauce over the clams and drizzle with a little olive oil to serve. Hand around the rest of the aïoli separately.

ROAST RUMP OF LAMB WITH HERB COUSCOUS

" The rump (or chump) of lamb is tender, sweet, and juicy—perfect for a quick, succulent roast. Our suppliers generally provide us with lovely thick rumps. Hopefully your butcher will do the same, but the rumps you are likely to find at your local supermarket will probably be thinner steaks. If you buy these, you'll need to reduce the cooking time slightly. "

6–8 servings

6–8 rumps of lamb, about 7oz (200g) each
few rosemary sprigs
4–5 garlic cloves, halved but not peeled
1 tbsp black peppercorns
olive oil, to drizzle
sea salt and freshly ground black pepper

HERB COUSCOUS:
2½ cups (600ml) lamb or chicken stock
1¾ cups (350g) couscous
2–3 tbsp Classic vinaigrette (see page 247)
large handful of parsley, leaves chopped
large handful of mint, leaves chopped
handful of cilantro, leaves chopped

TIP If you do not have a large enough ovenproof pan to take all the rumps, transfer them to a roasting pan after browning on the stove.

Lightly score the fat of the lamb in a criss-cross pattern. Place in a large dish and scatter over the rosemary, garlic, and peppercorns. Drizzle all over with olive oil and season with pepper. Cover with plastic wrap and let marinate in the refrigerator for at least 2 hours, preferably overnight.

Heat the oven to 400°F (200°C). Heat a large ovenproof pan on the stove. Remove the lamb rumps from the marinade, drain, and brown them in the hot pan in two or three batches for 2 to 3 minutes on each side. Return all the lamb to the pan and put into the oven for about 8 to 10 minutes to finish cooking. The rumps should feel slightly springy when pressed. Cover the lamb loosely with foil and set aside to rest in a warm place for 10 to 15 minutes before serving.

Prepare the couscous while the lamb is cooking. Bring the stock to the boil. Put the couscous into a large bowl and pour over the boiling stock. Cover the bowl with cling film and let soak for 10–15 minutes. Fluff up the couscous grains with a fork, drizzle over the vinaigrette, and season with salt and pepper to taste. Reserving a little for garnish, add the chopped herbs and fork through.

Slice the lamb thickly on the diagonal. Pile the herb couscous onto warm plates and arrange the lamb on top. Serve with the eggplant purée if you like, and sprinkle with the remaining herbs.

Spiced eggplant purée

Dice the eggplants, sprinkle lightly with sea salt, and put into a colander set over a bowl or the sink. Let drain for at least 30 minutes —the eggplants will release their bitter juices. Heat enough olive oil in a heavy deep pan for deep-frying (3–4 inch/7–10cm depth will be sufficient). Pat the eggplants dry with paper towels and deep-fry them, in several batches, until golden brown. Tip into a strainer set over a bowl and let drain off the excess oil or several hours, preferably overnight at room temperature.

Soak the golden raisins in a little boiling water or about 30 minutes. Heat a little olive oil in a pan, add the onions, and season with salt and pepper. Let sweat over medium-low heat, stirring occasionally, until lightly caramelized, about 15 to 20 minutes. Meanwhile, ightly score the top and bottom of the tomatoes with a cross and immerse in a bowl of boiling water for 30 seconds. Remove with a slotted spoon and refresh under cold running water. Peel off the skins, discard the seeds, and mince the tomato flesh.

Add the cumin to the caramelized onions and stir over medium heat for 2 to 3 minutes. Mix in the eggplants and tomatoes. Drain the golden raisins and add them to the pan to heat through. Tip the mixture into a blender or food processor and whiz to a purée. Return to the pan and season with salt and pepper to taste. Reheat the purée and stir through the chopped herbs before serving.

6–8 servings

2 large eggplants, trimmed
sea salt and freshly ground black pepper
olive oil, for deep-frying and cooking
scant ¼ cup (30g) golden raisins
5oz (150g) onions, peeled and chopped
3 ripe plum tomatoes
2 tsp ground cumin
handful of cilantro, leaves chopped
handful of basil, leaves chopped

TIP If you find the eggplant purée is too wet, stir it over high heat for a few minutes to cook off the excess moisture.

SUMMER PUDDING

66 Bursting with summer berries, this must be the crowning glory of English puddings. We often make individual puddings using brioche for a posh, restaurant-style dessert, but day-old slices of white bread are perfect for soaking up the juices from the berries. If using fresh bread, you may find it easier to firm up the bread in the refrigerator before slicing. 99

2¼lb (1kg) mixed berries, such as raspberries, blueberries, red currants, blackberries, and strawberries
¼ cup (50g) superfine sugar
4 tbsp crème de cassis (or water)
1 loaf of white bread (about 1¾lb/800g)
pouring cream, to serve

TIP Ripe, juicy berries are essential for this dessert. Halve or quarter any larger fruit, such as strawberries.

Toss all the berries

gently in a bowl with the sugar and cassis. Heat a nonstick pan until hot, then add the berries and liquor. Cook over medium heat for 1½ to 2 minutes until the fruit softens slightly and starts to bleed. Tip the fruit into a nonreactive strainer set over a nonmetallic bowl and allow the juices to drip through for 10 minutes.

Line an ovenproof bowl

(1.8-quart/1.8-liter) capacity or a similar-sized mixing bowl) with plastic wrap. Trim off the crusts from the bread and cut into ½-inch (1-cm) thick slices along the length of the loaf (rather than in the usual way). You will need about 5 or 6 long slices. Using a 3-inch (8-cm) round pastry cutter, stamp out a circle from one slice to line the base of the ovenproof bowl and another circle to cover the top (with an overlapping join if necessary). Trim the rest of the bread slices so they will fit around the sides, with a slight overlap. (Use any leftover bread to make fresh bread crumbs.)

Quickly dip one side

of the bread slices in the fruit syrup and use to line the bottom and sides of the bowl, placing the soaked side of the slices against the bowl. Spoon the fruit into the bowl, then dip the top bread slices into the juice and use to cover the fruit completely. Spoon the remaining juice over to soak the bread slices. Cover with plastic wrap, place a similar-sized saucer on top, and weigh down with a pan. Chill overnight.

When ready to serve,

remove the covering plastic wrap, then invert the pudding onto a rimmed plate. Remove the bowl and plastic wrap. Serve at the table, with a pitcher of pouring cream on the side.

"Who are you doing it with this Sunday?"

Classic Sunday lunch

There is nothing quite like a rib of beef for a traditional British Sunday lunch and with a little organization, you needn't spend all morning in the kitchen preparing the meal. As it is a substantial affair, you can easily forgo the appetizer. Substitute squab if pigeon is not available where you shop. This menu serves 4–6.

Pigeon salad with hazelnut vinaigrette

Roast beef with Yorkshire pudding & red wine gravy

+ Sautéed cabbage with caramelized onions
+ Glazed carrots with thyme & garlic
+ Roast potatoes with garlic & rosemary

Helen's Eve's pudding

planning your menu

A FEW DAYS AHEAD...
• Order the pigeon from your butcher or poulterer and get him to carve out the breasts. Reserve the rib of beef too.

THE DAY BEFORE...
• Make pie dough for the dessert and chill.

SEVERAL HOURS IN ADVANCE...
• Shape the pastry shell and chill. Make the apple filling.
• Make the dressing for the appetizer.
• Peel the potatoes and carrots and immerse in cold water.

TWO HOURS AHEAD...
• Bring the beef and pigeon breasts to room temperature.
• Bake the pastry shell and cool.
• Make the Yorkshire pudding batter.
• Prepare the salad ingredients for the appetizer, ready to assemble.

AN HOUR AHEAD...
• Put the beef into the oven to roast.
• Parboil the carrots.
• Blanch and refresh the cabbage and prepare the flavoring ingredients.
• Roast the potatoes.
• Assemble the eve's pudding ready for the meringue topping.

JUST BEFORE SERVING...
• Put the beef to rest and bake the Yorkshire puddings.
• Assemble the salad and pan-fry the pigeon. Plate the appetizer and serve.
• Take the Yorkshires out of the oven, lower the temperature (for the dessert).
• Finish cooking the vegetables, make the gravy, carve the beef, and serve the main course.
• Make the meringue topping for the dessert and bake. Let cool for a few minutes, then serve.

PIGEON SALAD WITH HAZELNUT VINAIGRETTE

66 We usually carve out the plump breasts and serve them pan-fried on a salad or a bed of lentils. This warm salad also makes a delicious light lunch. 99

4–6 servings

breasts from 8–12 large wood pigeons
sea salt and freshly ground black pepper
olive oil, for cooking
piece of butter
2 heads of oak leaf lettuce, washed
  and torn
4 large cooked beet, peeled and diced
½ cup (75g) roasted hazelnuts, lightly
  crushed
few wild arugula leaves (optional)

HAZELNUT VINAIGRETTE:
3½ tbsp (50ml) sherry vinegar
⅓ cup (100ml) olive oil
3½ tbsp (50ml) hazelnut oil

TIP If possible, get your butcher to carve out the pigeon breasts for you to save time. Ask for the carcasses—they will make a flavorful stock.

For the vinaigrette, whisk the ingredients together and season with salt and pepper to taste. Set aside.

Season the pigeon breasts with salt and pepper. Heat a heavy skillet with a little olive oil until hot. Add the pigeon breasts, skin side down, and cook for about 3 minutes until the skin is crisp. Turn them over and cook the other side for about 2 to 3 minutes, adding a piece of butter toward the end. As the butter melts, spoon it over the pigeon breasts to baste them. They should feel slightly springy when pressed. Transfer the pigeon breasts to a warm plate and let rest, lightly covered with foil, while you assemble the salad.

For the salad, toss the lettuce together with the beet, a handful of the crushed hazelnuts, and some of the vinaigrette. Divide the salad among individual plates.

Slice the pigeon breasts thickly into 4–5 even pieces. Drizzle a little vinaigrette over them to keep the meat moist. Arrange the pigeon breasts on top of the salad and scatter over the remaining hazelnuts. Drizzle over a little vinaigrette and finish with a few arugula leaves if you like.

ROAST BEEF
WITH YORKSHIRE PUDDING & RED WINE GRAVY

" According to photographer Jill's mum, you need 'love and hot fat' to make perfect crisp Yorkshire puddings...I can't argue with that! "

4–6 servings

2³⁄₄–3¹⁄₄lb (1.2–1.5kg) rib of beef, on the bone
sea salt and freshly ground black pepper
2 tbsp olive oil

YORKSHIRE PUDDINGS:
1²⁄₃ cups (225g) all-purpose flour
¹⁄₂ tsp salt
4 eggs, beaten
1¹⁄₄ cups (300ml) milk
about 4 tbsp vegetable oil (or beef drippings), for cooking

GRAVY:
few thyme sprigs
4 garlic cloves (unpeeled)
2 red onions, peeled and sliced
4 plum tomatoes, halved
¹⁄₂ bottle of red wine (about 1¹⁄₂ cups /350ml)
5 cups (1.2 liters) beef stock

Heat the oven to 400°F (200°C). Season the beef with salt and pepper and sear in a hot roasting pan with a little olive oil to brown on all sides, about 3 to 4 minutes on each side. Transfer to the oven and roast, allowing 15 minutes per 1lb (450g) for rare or 20 minutes per 1lb (450g) for medium.

For the Yorkshire batter, sift the flour and salt into a large bowl. Add the eggs and half the milk and beat until smooth. Mix in the remaining milk and let the batter rest.

When the beef is cooked, transfer to a warmed plate and let rest, lightly covered with foil, in a warm place while you cook the puddings and make the gravy. Increase the oven setting to 450°F (230°C). Put 1 tsp oil or, better still, hot fat from the beef roasting pan into each section of a 12-hole muffin tray (or Yorkshire pudding tray) and put into the oven on the top shelf until very hot (almost smoking).

Whisk the batter again in the meantime. As soon as you take the tray from the oven, ladle in the batter to three-quarters fill the pans (it should sizzle), and immediately put back into the oven. Bake for 15 to 20 minutes until the Yorkshire puddings are well risen, golden brown, and crisp. (Don't open the oven door until the end or they might collapse.)

To make the gravy, pour off excess fat from the roasting pan, place on medium heat and add the thyme, garlic, onions, and tomatoes. Cook for 4 to 5 minutes, then pour in the wine and bring to a simmer. Squash the tomatoes with a potato masher to thicken the sauce. Pour in the stock and bubble for 10 minutes until reduced by half. Pass the gravy through a strainer, pressing the vegetables to extract their flavor. Bring to a boil and reduce to a gravy consistency. Check the seasoning.

Carve the beef thinly. Serve with the gravy, Yorkshire puddings, sautéed cabbage, glazed carrots, and roast potatoes.

70

Sautéed cabbage with caramelized onions

4–6 servings

savoy cabbage, trimmed and shredded
red onions, peeled and sliced
olive oil, to drizzle
handful of sage leaves, chopped
piece of butter
sea salt and freshly ground black pepper

Blanch the cabbage

in a pan of boiling water for 2 minutes, drain, and refresh under cold running water, then drain well. Sweat the sliced onions in a pan with a little olive oil until softened and caramelized. Add the chopped sage and heat for another 2 to 3 minutes. Melt a piece of butter in a separate pan, add the cooked cabbage, and sauté for 3 to 4 minutes. Add the onion mixture and season with salt and pepper to taste. Sauté for another couple of minutes until the cabbage is tender and warmed through, then serve.

Glazed carrots with thyme & garlic

Put the carrots

into a large pan and pour over enough stock to cover. Add the thyme, garlic, and bay leaf and parboil for about 8 minutes (until the carrots are two-thirds cooked). Let the carrots cool in the stock, then drain thoroughly and pat dry. Heat a little olive oil in a sauté pan, add the carrots, and season well. Sauté for a couple of minutes, then add some butter and a sprinkling of sugar (for a caramelized finish). Baste the carrots with the melted butter and cook for another 3 to 4 minutes until they are tender and beautifully glazed.

4–6 servings

1⅓lb (600g) (18–20) small carrots, peeled
4–6 cups (1–1.5 liters) vegetable stock
1 thyme sprig
½ head of garlic (cut horizontally)
1 bay leaf
olive oil, for cooking
sea salt and freshly ground black pepper
few pieces of butter
1–2 tsp superfine sugar (optional)

Roast potatoes with garlic & rosemary

4–6 servings

2–3 tbsp vegetable oil or beef drippings
3lb 5oz (1.5kg) potatoes, such as Charlotte or round red, peeled
1 garlic clove, peeled and crushed
few rosemary sprigs
sea salt and freshly ground black pepper

Heat the oven

to 400°F (200°C). Put the oil in a sturdy baking tray on the stove over medium heat. When hot, add the potatoes and turn to coat well. Add the garlic and rosemary to the tray and season the potatoes well. Put the tray into the oven and roast, turning the potatoes occasionally, for 40 to 45 minutes until they are golden, crisp, and cooked through. Drain on paper towels and serve.

ELEN'S EVE'S PUDDING

" My mother's apple pudding is very different from mine and as far as she's concerned hers is definitely better! It has a sweet pie crust filled with stewed apples and topped with meringue, resembling a lemon meringue pie. It is best eaten soon after baking. **"**

4–6 servings

SWEET PIE DOUGH:
- ⅔ cup (150g) butter, softened to room temperature
- ½ cup (100g) superfine sugar
- 4 egg yolks, beaten
- 2¼ cups (300g) all-purpose flour, plus extra to dust
- pinch of salt

FILLING:
- 4 Granny Smith apples
- 2 tbsp superfine sugar

MERINGUE TOPPING:
- 2 egg whites
- 4 tbsp superfine sugar
- few drops of vanilla extract

To make the pie dough, cream together the butter and sugar, using a hand-held electric mixer until pale and creamy. Gradually add the egg yolks, then incorporate the flour and salt until the mixture is evenly blended and crumbly, adding 1–2 tbsp cold water if it seems too dry. Bring the dough together with your hand, press into a ball, flatten slightly, and wrap in plastic wrap. Chill for at least 30 minutes.

Roll out the dough thinly on a lightly floured surface and use to line an 8-inch (20-cm) tart pan with removable base. Line the dough with baking parchment or foil and fill with dried beans. Refrigerate for at least 20 minutes.

Make the filling in the meantime. Peel, core, and chop the apples and place in a pan with the sugar and 1 tbsp water. Cook gently for about 10 minutes until the apples are soft but still holding their shape. Tip onto a plate and let cool completely.

Heat the oven to 350°F (180°C). Bake the pastry shell blind for 15 minutes until golden at the edges, then remove the foil and beans and bake for another 5 minutes or until the base is cooked. Set aside to cool. Increase the oven setting to 400°F (200°C).

For the meringue, beat the egg whites, using a hand-held electric whisk until stiff. Gradually beat in the sugar, a spoonful at a time, with the vanilla until fully incorporated and the meringue is stiff.

Spread the apple filling in the pastry shell and top with the meringue. Peak the meringue with a fork to give it an attractive finish. Bake for 15 to 20 minutes until the meringue is golden brown. Cool slightly, then slice into individual portions and serve warm.

Red onion & sweet potato rösti
Serves 4–6

Heat a little olive oil in a wide heavy skillet and sauté 2 finely sliced red onions and 1 minced garlic clove for 5 minutes or until softened. Tip into a bowl and let cool. Peel and grate 1½lb (750g) sweet potatoes, wrap in a clean cloth, and squeeze out excess liquid. Mix with the sautéed onions, 1 medium beaten egg, 1 tbsp melted butter, and seasoning.

Heat a little olive oil and a piece of butter in a wide heavy skillet. Using one or more 4-inch (10-cm) greased plain metal cutters, shape the sweet potato mixture into neat cakes in the skillet, pressing the mixture down in the rings. Cook over medium-low heat for about 5 to 6 minutes until the underside is golden brown, then remove the rings and flip the rösti with a spatula. Cook the other side for 2 to 3 minutes until crisp. Drain the rösti on paper towels and keep warm while cooking the remaining mixture. Equally good with meat, chicken, and vegetables dishes.

Duchess potatoes
Serves 4–6

Heat the oven to 425°F (220°C). Peel 3¼lb (1.5kg) mealy potatoes (such as Russet) and halve or quarter if large. Boil in salted water for 12 to 15 minutes until tender. Drain, then return to the pan and place over low heat for a minute or so to drive off excess moisture. Mash the potatoes well, using a potato ricer if possible. For a smoother finish, push the mash through a fine strainer.

Return the mashed potatoes to the pan and place over medium heat. Stir in ⅔ cup (150g) butter and season with salt, pepper, and a little grated nutmeg if you like. Take the pan off the heat and mix in 2 beaten medium eggs. Spoon the enriched mash into a large pastry bag fitted with a ¾-inch (2-cm) fluted tip and, while still warm, pipe into whirls on a greased baking sheet. Bake for 5 to 7 minutes until golden and crisp at the edges. An elegant accompaniment to meat, poultry, game, or fish.

Roast Charlotte potatoes with chorizo
Serves 4–6

Heat the oven to 400°F (200°C). Boil 2¼lb (1kg) medium Charlotte potatoes in salted water for 7 to 9 minutes. Drain and peel when cool enough to handle, then cut in half. Chop 7oz (200g) fresh (or smoked) chorizo sausage into bite-size pieces. Heat a thin layer of olive oil in an ovenproof skillet, add the chorizo, and sauté until it starts to release oil. Toss in the potatoes, season well, then roast in the oven for 15 to 20 minutes until golden brown. Sprinkle with chopped parsley. Delicious with Mediterranean-style chicken and fish.

Sautéed potatoes with paprika
Serves 4–6

Scrub 2¼lb (1kg) Charlotte (or other waxy) potatoes and boil in salted water for 7 to 9 minutes. Drain and peel while still hot (wearing rubber gloves). Cut the potatoes into ½-inch (1-cm) cubes and drizzle with a little olive oil. Spread out on a tray, season well, and let cool. Heat a little olive oil in a wide skillet over medium-high heat. Add the diced potatoes and cook, turning occasionally, until golden brown, crisp at the edges, and tender. Drain on paper towels. Serve warm, sprinkled with mild paprika and sea salt. Lovely with fish or poultry dishes.

Champ with scallions & fava beans
Serves 4–6

Peel 3¼lb (1.5kg) mealy potatoes and halve or quarter if large. Boil in salted water for 12 to 15 minutes until tender; drain well. Mash the potatoes while still hot, then stir through 4 tbsp butter. Bring a scant 2 cups (450ml) milk and ⅔ cup (150ml) heavy cream to a boil in another pan. Add 5–6 minced scallions and 2⅔ cups (400g) shelled fava beans and cook for 2 minutes until the beans are tender. Transfer the onions and beans to the potatoes, then gradually stir in enough of the creamy milk to achieve a good texture. Season. Reheat, stir through a handful of chopped chives and top with a piece of butter. Perfect with rustic stews or braised meat dishes.

08 Keep it simple

Fine fish is a smart choice for an impressive quick main course. Follow with a heavenly dessert and everyone will be more than satisfied. Make the appetizer ahead or for an easy last-minute option, serve Asparagus with herb butter (see page 43). This menu serves 6.

Piquant mushroom & vegetable salad

Black bream with basil & peas "bonne femme"

Cherry clafoutis

planning your menu

A FEW DAYS AHEAD...
• Order the fish from the fish supplier (get him to fillet it for you). Arrange to collect it on the day if possible, or the day before.

THE DAY BEFORE...
• Prepare the marinated mushrooms for the appetizer and refrigerate overnight.
• Make the clafoutis batter, pit the cherries, and chill.

AN HOUR IN ADVANCE...
• For the peas "bonne femme", peel the onions and pod fresh peas if using.
• Bring the clafoutis batter to room temperature and divide the cherries among baking dishes, ready to cook.
• For the appetizer, blanch the vegetables for the appetizer and toss in the vinaigrette.
• Prepare the fish fillets and wrap in plastic wrap, ready to cook.

HALF AN HOUR AHEAD...
• Take the mushrooms out of the refrigerator.
• For the peas, cook the bacon and onions; set aside.
• Pour the batter over the cherries and bake the clafoutis.

JUST BEFORE SERVING...
• Assemble the appetizer.
• Poach the bream fillets while you eat your appetizer, timing carefully.
• Finish the peas "bonne femme" and assemble the main course.
• Leave the clafoutis at room temperature while you eat the main course.
• Dust the cherry clafoutis with confectioners' sugar and serve.

PIQUANT MUSHROOM & VEGETABLE SALAD

" I first came across this salad at a restaurant in Paris and I was intrigued by the flavorings used for the mushrooms, all coming together in a sweet-and-sour medley of summer vegetables. The whole coriander seeds provide an invigorating twist to the salad but you can just use ground coriander if you find the seeds too harsh. "

6 servings

MARINATED MUSHROOMS:
2 tbsp raisins
2 tbsp golden raisins
1⅓lb (600g) white mushrooms, cleaned
4 tbsp olive oil
1 large onion, peeled and chopped
1 tsp whole coriander seeds
2 tsp ground coriander
sea salt and freshly ground black pepper
1¼ cups (300ml) dry white wine
1 bouquet garni (parsley stalks, celery, thyme sprigs, and a bay leaf)
juice of ½ lemon, or to taste
4 large ripe tomatoes, about 1lb (500g) in total
1 tbsp tomato paste
pinch of superfine sugar, or to taste

SALAD:
½ head of cauliflower, cut into florets
7oz (200g) baby leeks, white part only, trimmed
5oz (150g) pearl onions, peeled
9oz (250g) small asparagus tips
2 cups (200g) fresh or frozen peas (thawed if frozen)
4 tbsp Classic vinaigrette (see page 247)
handful of mint leaves, shredded

Put the dried fruit in a small bowl, add boiling water to cover and let soak for at least 20 minutes, then drain. Twist the stems off the mushrooms and cut any larger ones in half.

Heat the olive oil in a large pan. Add the onion with the coriander seeds, ground coriander, and some seasoning and cook gently for 5 minutes or until starting to soften. Add the white wine and bouquet garni. Boil for 7 to 10 minutes until reduced by half, then lower the heat. Add the mushrooms and lemon juice, cover, and sweat for 5 minutes.

Score the tomatoes, top and bottom, with a cross and immerse in a bowl of boiling water for 40 seconds. Remove, refresh under cold water, then peel off the skins. Halve and seed, then put into a food processor with the tomato paste and whiz until smooth.

Transfer the mushrooms to a strainer set over a bowl to drain, using a slotted spoon. Tip the puréed tomatoes into the mushroom liquor and boil over high heat for 7 to 10 minutes until thickened, stirring frequently. Discard the bouquet garni. Return the mushrooms to the pan and add the raisins and golden raisins. Reheat for a few minutes. Check the seasoning and balance the acidity with a pinch of sugar or a little more lemon juice. Transfer to a bowl to cool, then cover and refrigerate overnight to allow the flavors to mingle.

Take the mushrooms out of the refrigerator half an hour before serving. For the salad, blanch the vegetables separately in boiling salted water for about 2 to 3 minutes. Drain, refresh in iced water, and drain well, then tip into a large bowl and dress with the vinaigrette. Add the mushrooms and tomato marinade and toss to combine. Serve with a generous sprinkling of shredded mint.

BLACK BREAM
WITH BASIL & PEAS "BONNE FEMME"

" Black bream has a delicate, slightly sweet flavor that really comes through when the fish is gently poached or steamed. French-style peas with snippets of bacon and little onions are the perfect base for the fish. "

6 servings

6 black bream fillets, skin on, about
  6oz (175g) each
sea salt and freshly ground black pepper
small handful of basil leaves
olive oil, to drizzle

PEAS "BONNE FEMME:"
olive oil, for cooking
9oz (250g) unsmoked bacon, cut into small
  cubes
5oz (150g) pearl onions, peeled
few thyme sprigs, leaves only
1⅓lb (600g) fresh or frozen peas
  (thawed, if frozen)

TIP At our restaurants, we wrap the fish and herbs in plastic wrap before poaching, to seal in the juices and prevent the fish from becoming waterlogged. if you're not comfortable with the idea of cooking in plastic wrap, steaming would achieve a comparable result.

Check the fish for small bones, removing any that you find with tweezers. Score the skin at ½-inch (1-cm) intervals. Season with salt and pepper and place a few basil leaves on the flesh side. Place each bream fillet on a large piece of plastic wrap and drizzle with olive oil. Wrap up to enclose the fillets in the plastic wrap, twisting the ends tightly to seal.

For the peas, heat a little olive oil in a skillet and cook the bacon for 8 to 10 minutes until golden brown and crisp. Remove and drain on paper towels. Add the onions and thyme to the pan and cook on medium heat, stirring occasionally, for 10 minutes until the onions are tender.

In the meantime, bring a large pan of water to a boil, then reduce the heat to a low simmer. Add the wrapped bream fillets and gently poach for about 10 minutes until the fish is opaque and cooked through. If the center is not cooked through, poach for another 2 to 3 minutes.

Add the peas and bacon to the onions and cook for 2 to 3 minutes until the peas are tender. Season well.

Divide the peas "bonne femme" among six warm plates. Unwrap the bream fillets and place on top of the vegetables, skin side up. Drizzle with a little olive oil and sprinkle with sea salt. Serve immediately.

CHERRY CLAFOUTIS

" To the French, cherry clafoutis is what bread and butter pudding is to the British—a real comfort pudding that has stood the test of time. When fresh cherries are out of season, we often use bottled cherries marinated in kirsch to make clafoutis. "

6 servings

½ cup (50g) ground almonds
1 tbsp (15g) all-purpose flour
generous pinch of fine sea salt
½ cup (100g) superfine sugar
2 large eggs
3 large egg yolks
1 cup (250ml) heavy cream
unsalted butter, to grease
confectioners' sugar, to dust
10oz (300g) fresh cherries, washed and
   pitted

TIP The clafoutis batter can be made in a food processor. Pulse the dry ingredients for a few seconds to combine, then add the eggs and cream and whiz until smooth.

Put the ground almonds, flour, salt, and sugar into a large bowl and mix well to combine. Make an indentation in the center. In another bowl, beat the eggs, egg yolks, and cream together, then pour into the hollow in the dry mixture. Whisk until the batter is smooth. If preparing in advance, transfer the batter to a pitcher (or cover the bowl with plastic wrap) and chill overnight.

Heat the oven to 375°F (190°C). Generously butter 4–6 shallow ovenproof dishes and dust the base and sides with confectioners' sugar. Divide the pitted cherries among the prepared dishes. Give the batter a stir, then pour over the cherries. Place the dishes on a large baking sheet and bake in the oven for 20 to 30 minutes until golden brown and risen. Check that the clafoutis have set in the middle, if not bake for another 5 minutes.

Let the clafoutis stand for 5 to 10 minutes. Add a dusting of confectioners' sugar before serving.

NEARLY 10% OF PEOPLE USE FROZEN OR PREPREPARED FOOD EVERY DAY OF THE WEEK.

"Using fresh ingredients is the only way to guarantee a great taste. I can't understand how on earth people can ignore fresh food. That's where all the flavor is, all the goodness, and it's a crime not to use it. Fresh food is what your family should be eating and if it means shopping more frequently or traveling to a couple of markets, then trust me, it's worth it."

09 Easy barbecue

Perfect for a summer barbecue, this food is equally good cooked indoors on a griddle or under the broiler, so you're not dependant on the weather. For a more substantial meal, add sausages and Griddled chicken (see page 162). This menu serves 6–8.

Crushed peas & mozzarella on toast with romano

Honey mustard pork chops

Ginger & port marinated lamb skewers

+ New potato salad

+ Green bean, spinach & red onion salad

Blueberry & red currant Eton mess

(see page 162)

planning your menu

THE DAY BEFORE...
- Marinate the meats in the refrigerator overnight.
- Make the meringues for the dessert (unless using ready-made).

SEVERAL HOURS IN ADVANCE...
- For the appetizer, prepare the crushed peas, cover, and set aside.
- Make the dressing for the potato salad and wash the potatoes ready for cooking.

TWO HOURS AHEAD...
- Blanch the beans and prepare the other salad ingredients, ready to assemble.
- Make the berry purée for the dessert.

ABOUT HALF AN HOUR AHEAD...
- Whip the cream and crush the meringues, so the dessert is all ready to assemble.
- Drain the lamb and thread onto kebab skewers. Prepare chops for cooking.
- Cook the potatoes and toss with the dressing while hot.
- Prepare the green bean salad.

JUST BEFORE SERVING...
- Assemble the appetizer and serve your guests, while you start cooking the meat on the barbecue or griddle.
- Serve the barbecued meats with the salads.
- Assemble the dessert and serve.

CRUSHED PEAS & MOZZARELLA ON TOAST WITH ROMANO

66 These little bites are a take on bruschetta, with a summery aspect from the green peas. You could take the dish a step further by blending the peas with the leaves from a bunch of mint or Italian parsley, which will turn the crushed peas a deeper shade of green. 99

6–8 servings

3½ cups (400g) shelled fresh peas
sea salt and freshly ground black pepper
½ cup (125g) mascarpone
4 tbsp olive oil, plus extra to drizzle
12–16 thick slices of ciabatta
4oz (100g) bocconcini (baby mozzarella)
4 tbsp freshly grated romano

Cook the peas in boiling salted water for 3 to 5 minutes until they are really tender, then drain and tip into a food processor. Add the mascarpone, olive oil, and seasoning and whiz to a rough paste. Transfer to a bowl and set aside.

Preheat a griddle or broiler until hot. Toast the ciabatta slices for about 2 minutes on each side, then drizzle with a little olive oil.

Spread the crushed peas on the toasted ciabatta slices. Roughly tear the mozzarella balls in half and place on top. Sprinkle with the romano and drizzle with a little more olive oil. Grind over a little more seasoning and serve immediately.

TIP You'll need approximately 2lb (1kg) peas in the pod to give this shelled weight.

HONEY MUSTARD PORK CHOPS

" These tasty chops—and the lamb skewers below—are two of my favorite things to cook on a barbecue or griddle. The marinades not only tenderize the meat, they also impart great flavors. "

6–8 servings

6–8 pork chops, about 7oz (200g) each
olive oil, to brush

MARINADE:
2 tbsp Dijon mustard
4 tbsp wholegrain mustard
6 tbsp runny honey
4 tbsp Worcestershire sauce
4 tbsp light soy sauce

Mix the marinade ingredients together in shallow bowl. Add the pork chops and turn to coat well. Cover with plastic wrap and marinate in the refrigerator for a few hours or overnight.

Heat a griddle pan, barbecue (or broiler) until hot. Scrape the excess marinade off the pork chops and save it. Brush the chops with a little olive oil. Cook on the barbecue, griddle (or broiler) for 4 to 5 minutes on each side or until cooked through, basting with the marinade. Rest the chops in a warm spot for 5 to 10 minutes (while you cook the lamb).

Serve the pork chops with the lamb skewers or other barbecued meats, accompanied by side salads and crusty bread.

GINGER & PORT MARINATED LAMB SKEWERS

6–8 servings

8–10 wooden kebab skewers
1¾lb (800g) boneless tender lamb
olive oil, to brush

MARINADE:
¾ cup (200ml) port
2 tbsp grated fresh gingerroot
4 garlic cloves, peeled and crushed
few rosemary sprigs, bruised with
   the back of a knife
sea salt and freshly ground black pepper
2 tbsp olive oil

Soak the kebab skewers in cold water. Combine the port, ginger, garlic, and rosemary in a wide shallow bowl. Cut the lamb into ¾-inch (2-cm) cubes, add to the bowl, and turn to coat in the marinade. Cover with plastic wrap and let marinate in the refrigerator for 3 to 4 hours or overnight (no longer, otherwise the port will overpower the flavor of the lamb).

Drain the lamb and pat dry with paper towels. Season the meat and brush with a little olive oil, then thread onto the skewers. Cook on a preheated barbecue or griddle (or broiler) for about 2 to 3 minutes on each side. The lamb should be slightly springy when pressed.

New potato salad

Cook the potatoes
in boiling salted water for 8 to 10 minutes or until just tender. In the meantime, whisk the dressing ingredients together, seasoning with salt and pepper to taste. When cooked, drain the potatoes and place in a mixing bowl with the shallot and chopped mint. While the potatoes are still hot, add the dressing and toss to mix. Serve warm or at room temperature.

6–8 servings

2¼lb (1kg) baby new potatoes, washed
sea salt and freshly ground black pepper
1 large shallot, peeled and minced
handful of mint or tarragon, leaves chopped

DRESSING:
1 tbsp tarragon vinegar or cider vinegar
2 tsp Dijon mustard
1 tsp wholegrain mustard
2 tbsp olive oil
2 tbsp walnut oil
2 tsp runny honey

Green bean, spinach & red onion salad

6–8 servings

10oz (300g) green beans, trimmed
sea salt and freshly ground black pepper
3 red onions, peeled and very thinly sliced
1lb 2oz (500g) baby spinach leaves,
   washed and spun dry

DRESSING:
3 tbsp balsamic vinegar
⅓ cup (100ml) olive oil

Blanch the beans
in a pan of boiling salted water for 2 minutes. Drain and refresh under cold running water. Drain the beans well and tip them into a large bowl. Add the sliced red onions and spinach leaves and toss to mix. Whisk the balsamic vinegar and olive oil together with some seasoning to make the dressing. Pour this over the salad and toss well just before serving.

BLUEBERRY & RED CURRANT ETON MESS

" A scrumptious muddle of berries and cream originating from the boarding school of the same name. I often make it for my children, using berries we've picked ourselves. Add the crushed meringues just before serving, to keep them light and crisp. "

⅔ cups (300g) red currants, plus
  sprigs to finish
cups (300g) blueberries
tbsp superfine sugar, plus extra to coat
tbsp kirsch (optional)
½ cups (600ml) heavy cream
  tbsp confectioners' sugar
meringue nests (ideally homemade,
  see page 248)

Put half the fruit
into a dry nonstick pan with the sugar and kirsch if using. Cook over high heat for 1½ to 2 minutes until the berries soften and begin to bleed. Crush lightly with a fork and push the fruit through a nonreactive strainer into a large bowl. Let cool completely.

Whip the cream
together with the confectioners' sugar in another bowl until it forms soft peaks. Crush the meringue nests and fold them through the cream with the remaining berries. Fold or ripple through the cooled berry coulis.

Spoon the mixture
into a large glass bowl or onto individual serving plates. Coat the remaining red currants with a little superfine sugar and use to decorate each plate.

93

10 Seafood special

Monkfish is teamed with mussels for a stylish seafood meal. A creamy risotto makes a lovely fall appetizer, or you might prefer to extend the seafood theme and start with Roasted tomato salad with shrimp and anchovies (see page 229). For a lighter dessert, I recommend my Lemon tart (see page 137). This menu serves 4–6.

Pumpkin risotto with Parmesan
Monkfish with curried mussels
Ginger chocolate cheesecake

planning your menu

A FEW DAYS AHEAD...
• Order the monkfish from your fish supplier and get him to fillet it for you. Arrange to pick it up on the day if possible, or the day before.

THE DAY BEFORE...
• Make the cheesecake and the flavored crème fraîche and chill.

SEVERAL HOURS IN ADVANCE...
• Make the pumpkin purée for the risotto.

TWO HOURS AHEAD...
• Clean the mussels.

AN HOUR AHEAD...
• Trim the monkfish and set aside at room temperature.
• Prepare and chop the vegetables for the main course.
• Cook and shell the mussels.

30 MINUTES AHEAD...
• Sauté the main course vegetables and reduce the liquor. Dust the monkfish with the curry/salt mix, ready to cook.
• Cook the risotto.

JUST BEFORE SERVING...
• Plate the risotto and serve.
• Pan-fry the monkfish, wilt the spinach, finish the main course, and serve.
• Unmold the cheesecake, slice, and serve with the ginger crème fraîche.

PUMPKIN RISOTTO WITH PARMESAN

" I love making this risotto toward the end of fall when pumpkins are ripe and flavorful. We usually cook with iron bark pumpkins at the restaurant—jack o'lantern Halloween pumpkins are too watery and stringy. You can use butternut squash, allowing a little longer for it to cook. "

4–6 servings

large wedge of ripe pumpkin, about 1lb 2oz–1⅓lb (500–600g)
olive oil, for cooking and to drizzle
5½ cups (1.3 liters) Chicken (or vegetable) stock (see page 246)
1⅓ cups (300g) risotto rice (Arborio or Carnaroli)
sea salt and freshly ground black pepper
few pieces of butter
2oz (50g) Parmesan, freshly grated, plus shavings to serve
small handful of sage leaves

TIP Cooked pumpkin purée freezes well, so if you find yourself having to buy a whole pumpkin that's more than you need, cook and purée the lot, freezing the rest for later use.

Cut the pumpkin
into ½-inch (1-cm) cubes. Heat a little olive oil in a large pan over medium heat. Add the pumpkin and cook gently for 5 to 7 minutes until just softened, stirring occasionally. Set aside one-third. Put the rest of the pumpkin into a blender and whiz until smooth, adding a touch of hot water as necessary (to get the purée moving in the blender).

Bring the stock
to a simmer in a pan and keep it at a gentle simmer over low heat. Heat a little olive oil in a larger pan and tip in the rice. Cook, stirring frequently, for a minute, then add a ladleful of hot stock and stir until it is almost all absorbed before adding another ladleful. Repeat until you've reached your last few ladlefuls of stock. Taste the rice to see if it is *al dente*. If not, add more stock. Add the pumpkin purée and reserved pumpkin, stirring through and seasoning to taste. Stir in a few pieces of butter and the grated Parmesan. Keep warm.

Heat a thin layer of olive oil
in a small skillet until hot. Sauté the sage leaves for a few seconds until crisp then drain on paper towels.

Ladle the risotto
onto warm plates and tap the bottom of each plate gently to spread it out. Drizzle with a little olive oil and scatter over the Parmesan and sage leaves, then serve.

MONKFISH WITH CURRIED MUSSELS

❝ I love this combination. A light coating of curry spice gives the monkfish a golden crust and imparts a subtle taste that doesn't overpower the delicate flavor of the fish. There's plenty going on here, so you don't really need any accompaniments, though you could serve Pommes purée (see page 43) on the side if you like. ❞

4–6 servings

4–6 monkfish tail fillets, about 5oz (150g) each
1lb 2oz (500g) mussels, cleaned with beards removed
few thyme sprigs
2 bay leaves
5 tbsp (75ml) dry white wine
1 large carrot, peeled and chopped
1 leek, trimmed and chopped
½ celeriac, peeled and chopped
3 tbsp olive oil
5 tsp curry powder
2 pinches of saffron strands
sea salt and freshly ground black pepper
14oz (400g) baby spinach, washed
piece of butter
¾ cup (200ml) heavy cream
handful of chives, chopped

Trim the monkfish fillets if necessary, removing any gray membrane. Heat the oven to 350°F (180°C).

Heat a large pan until hot, then add the mussels, a couple of thyme sprigs, the bay leaves, and white wine. Cover the pan with a tight-fitting lid and give it a good shake. Cook for about 3 to 4 minutes, shaking once or twice, until the mussels have opened. Strain and set aside the juices. Remove the mussels from their shells and set aside; discard any unopened ones.

Sauté the vegetables in 1 tbsp olive oil until soft. Sprinkle with 1 tsp curry powder and the saffron. Add a thyme sprig, tip in the mussel juice, and simmer until reduced by half.

Meanwhile, mix the remaining 4 tsp curry powder with 1 tsp salt. Pat the monkfish tails dry with paper towels and dust with the curry/salt mix. Heat 2 tbsp olive oil in an ovenproof skillet and cook the monkfish fillets for 2 to 3 minutes until golden brown. Transfer the pan to the oven for 4 to 5 minutes to finish off the cooking. The fish is ready when it feels just firm.

Wilt the spinach gently in a warm pan with a piece of butter for about 1 to 2 minutes while the fish is in the oven. At the same time, pour the cream into the sautéed vegetables and bring to a gentle simmer. Add the mussels to warm through, then finally mix in the chives and season to taste.

Divide the spinach among warm plates and spoon over the creamy mussel mixture. Thickly slice the monkfish and arrange on top. Serve at once.

GINGER CHOCOLATE CHEESECAKE

66 This cheesecake, made by firefighter Paul Beer on the first F word series, proved to be more popular than mine! I have to confess it has just the right balance of sweetness and bitterness from the semisweet chocolate, with a subtle hint of ginger. Baked cheesecakes characteristically sink when they cool so don't be alarmed to see cracks on the surface of your cheesecake. 99

6–8 servings

5oz (150g) preserved ginger cookies, broken up
4 tbsp (50g) unsalted butter, melted, plus extra to grease
generous 1 cup (250g) mascarpone
scant 1 cup (200g) fromage frais
2 large eggs
3 tbsp (35g) superfine sugar
5oz (150g) semisweet chocolate with preserved ginger, broken into pieces

TO SERVE:
¾ cup (200g) crème fraîche
1 tbsp preserved ginger syrup
5 pieces candied preserved ginger (or 2 pieces preserved ginger from the jar)
confectioners' sugar, to dust

Heat the oven to 375°F (190°C). Put the cookies into a food processor and blitz to fine crumbs. Tip into a bowl and mix with the melted butter. Pour the mixture into a lightly greased 8-inch (20-cm) round cake pan with a removable base and level out with the back of a spatula or a large spoon. Bake for 5 minutes, then set aside to cool. Lower the oven setting to 325°F (170°C).

Whisk the mascarpone and fromage frais together in a bowl until smooth. Add the eggs and sugar and mix well. Melt the chocolate in a bain-marie (or bowl set over a pan of barely simmering water) and then gently fold into the mascarpone mixture.

Pour the filling over the cookie base and bake for 50 to 60 minutes. The cheesecake is ready when the filling is just set—it should still have a slight wobble in the center. Remove from the oven and run a thin knife around the edge of the pan. Let the cheesecake cool in the pan, during which time the filling will continue to set.

Before serving, flavor the crème fraîche with the ginger syrup, folding it in until evenly blended. Finely slice the ginger into thin sticks. Carefully unmold the cheesecake onto a plate. Serve cut into slices with the ginger crème fraîche, a scattering of ginger, and a dusting of confectioners' sugar.

11 Roast lamb

This enticing menu captures some wonderful flavors of spring—red mullet, new season's lamb, and tender rhubarb. If you would rather serve a prepare-ahead appetizer, Horseradish marinated salmon (see page 181) is a good option. This menu serves 6.

Red mullet with sautéed potatoes & anchovy dressing

Saddle of lamb with apricot & cumin stuffing

+ Spinach with garlic, chile & pine nuts

+ Balsamic roasted red onions

+ Pommes purée (see page 43)

Rhubarb crème brûlée

planning your menu

A FEW DAYS AHEAD...
• Order the saddle of lamb from your butcher and the fish from the fish supplier (arranging to collect a day ahead, or pick the mullet up fresh on the day if you can).

THE DAY BEFORE...
• Make the stuffing and prepare the lamb so it's stuffed, rolled, tied, and all ready to roast. Wrap in plastic wrap and refrigerate.
• Make the crème brûlées and chill, ready to apply the topping the next day.

SEVERAL HOURS IN ADVANCE...
• Check the fish fillets for pin bones; keep in the refrigerator. Prepare the dressing, saving the tarragon to add at the last minute.
• Prepare and cook the balsamic onions, ready to reheat before serving (unless you have a second oven to cook them in at the same time as the meat).
• Peel the potatoes for the pommes purée and immerse in cold water.

TWO HOURS AHEAD...
• Bring the meat to room temperature.
• Wash the spinach and prepare the flavoring ingredients ready to cook.
• For the appetizer, parboil the potatoes, peel (but don't slice) and toss in olive oil.

FROM AN HOUR AHEAD...
• Take the red mullet from the refrigerator and score it. Slice the parboiled potatoes and finish the dressing.
• Sear the lamb and put it into the oven to roast. Prepare and cook the pommes purée; keep warm.

JUST BEFORE SERVING...
• Sauté the potatoes, pan-fry the fish, and assemble the appetizer.
• Rest the meat and reheat the onions while you eat the appetizer.
• Sauté the spinach, carve the lamb, and serve the main course.
• Finish the crème brûlées and serve.

RED MULLET
WITH SAUTEED POTATOES & ANCHOVY DRESSING

"" Really fresh fish needs nothing more than quick, simple cooking. My favorite way of cooking fish fillets is pan-frying, which leaves the fish with a beautifully crisp skin and succulent flesh. Here, pan-fried red mullet is served with sautéed potatoes and an uplifting anchovy dressing, guaranteed to wake up the taste buds. **""**

6 servings

1½lb (750g) even-size Charlotte
  potatoes, washed
sea salt and freshly ground black pepper
olive oil, for cooking
12 red mullet fillets, about 4oz (100g)
  each, skin on
large handful of frisée leaves

ANCHOVY DRESSING:
2oz (50g) can anchovy fillets, drained
1 garlic clove, peeled and crushed
1 tbsp white wine vinegar
⅓ cup (100ml) olive oil
1 tsp chopped tarragon

Boil the potatoes in a pan of salted water for 7 minutes, drain, and briefly refresh under cold running water. While still warm, peel off the skins and cut the potatoes into thick ¾-inch (2-cm) slices.

Heat a sauté pan with a thin film of olive oil. Add the potato slices, season well, and cook over medium heat for about 5 minutes on each side until golden brown and cooked through.

For the anchovy dressing, put the anchovies, garlic, and wine vinegar into a food processor and whiz to a rough purée. With the motor running, slowly trickle in the olive oil until amalgamated. Transfer the dressing to a bowl and stir in the tarragon.

Check the fish fillets for small pin bones, removing any you find with tweezers. Score the skin at ½-inch (1-cm) intervals. Heat a wide skillet until hot and add a little olive oil. Season the fish fillets and place them in the hot pan, skin side down. Cook for 2 to 3 minutes until the skin is crisp and the fish is cooked two-thirds of the way through, then turn over and cook the other side for 30 seconds. Lift the fish onto a warm plate.

Arrange the sautéed potatoes in the center of six warm serving plates. Place two fish fillets on top of each portion and scatter the frisée leaves around the plate. Spoon over the anchovy dressing and serve immediately.

SADDLE OF LAMB WITH APRICOT & CUMIN STUFFING

" A saddle of lamb comes with two loins, from both sides of the backbone, and once the bone is removed, there is a natural cavity that is perfect for stuffing and rolling. Get your butcher to skin and bone the saddle for you and ask for the bones to make stock. The roasted cumin, apricot, and pine nut stuffing is superb with the sweet, tender lamb. "

6 servings

3lb (1.3kg) saddle of lamb, skinned
   and boned
2 tbsp cumin seeds
sea salt and freshly ground black pepper
20–22 slices of prosciutto, about 7oz
   (200g) in total
sea salt and freshly ground black pepper
olive oil, for cooking

STUFFING:
scant 1 cup (150g) apricots, soaked
   overnight in warm water, drained
scant ¼ cup (30g) pine nuts, toasted
½ cup (25g) fresh bread crumbs
1 tbsp olive oil

TIP Any extra stuffing can be formed into balls, rolled in bread crumbs, and roasted alongside the lamb for the last 20 minutes or so.

Trim off the excess fillets at both ends of the saddle so that you can roll the lamb into a neat log. (Use them for another dish.) Toast the cumin seeds in a hot dry pan, tossing occasionally, until fragrant. Using a mortar and pestle, coarsely grind the seeds with a pinch each of sea salt and pepper, then rub half over the lamb.

For the stuffing, mince the apricots and pine nuts (or pulse in a food processor to a rough paste), then tip into a bowl. Stir in the bread crumbs, olive oil, some salt and pepper, and the rest of the cumin.

On a large sheet of plastic wrap, arrange all but two of the prosciutto slices in a rectangle, overlapping them slightly. (This needs to be large enough to wrap around the lamb.) Lay the lamb, opened out like a butterfly, on top of the prosciutto. Season the lamb and pile the stuffing in a neat row along the center. (You may not need all of it.) Fold the sides of the lamb over the stuffing. Wrap the lamb package in the prosciutto and outer plastic wrap to form a tight log. Chill for an hour to slightly "set" the shape.

Heat the oven to 350°F (180°C). Remove the plastic wrap from the lamb. Use the remaining slices of prosciutto to cover the two ends and secure the stuffing. Tie the log with kitchen string at ¾–1¼ inch (2–3cm) intervals—just firmly enough to hold it together during roasting.

Heat a little olive oil in a wide ovenproof skillet until hot. Sear the lamb for 3 to 4 minutes on each side until browned, then position seam side down in the center of the pan and transfer to the oven. Roast for 35 to 40 minutes, turning and basting the lamb halfway through cooking. It should feel slightly springy when pressed and the meat should be pink in the center. Rest in a warm place for 10 to 15 minutes, then slice thickly and serve with the pan juices and accompaniments.

Spinach with garlic, chile & pine nuts

Sauté the garlic in a little olive oil in a wide pan for a minute until golden brown, then add the chile and pine nuts. Toss over medium heat until the nuts are nicely toasted and golden brown. Add the spinach leaves in large handfuls, stirring and wilting each handful before adding the next one. Season well and serve at once.

6 servings

3 garlic cloves, peeled and finely sliced
olive oil, for cooking
½ red chile seeded and minced
⅓ cup (50g) pine nuts
1½lb (750g) baby spinach, washed
sea salt and freshly ground black pepper

Balsamic roasted red onions

6 servings

6–8 medium red onions
1½ tbsp (20g) unsalted butter
1 tbsp olive oil
few rosemary sprigs
sea salt and freshly ground black pepper
5 tbsp balsamic vinegar

Heat the oven to 275°F (140°C). Peel the onions and slice off one-third of the tops to expose the layers. Heat the butter and olive oil in a heavy ovenproof pan. Add the onions, cut side down, and sauté for 4 to 5 minutes until golden brown. Add the rosemary and season the onions with salt and pepper. Deglaze the pan with the balsamic vinegar, cover with foil, and transfer to the oven.

Slowly roast the onions for 30 minutes, then remove the foil and turn the onions cut side up. Return the pan to the oven for 1 to 1¼ hours until the onions are tender. Check halfway through as you may need to add a few tablespoonfuls of water if the balsamic vinegar evaporates away. To test if the onions are ready, pierce the middle of the thickest one with a small knife—it should meet with little resistance. Spoon the syrupy glaze over the onions and serve warm.

RHUBARB CREME BRULEE

66 Crème brûlée was one of the first desserts I learned to perfect while working under Guy Savoy in Paris. I like to add different flavors to this classic French custard and rhubarb is one of my favorites. Chopped rhubarb is sautéed with honey and vanilla then baked under the creamy custard. As it cooks gently in the oven, the softened rhubarb infuses with the creamy custard to delicious effect. 99

6 servings

1½ tbsp (20g) butter
7oz (200g) rhubarb, trimmed and
 chopped
4 tbsp honey
1 vanilla bean, split
1¼ cups (300ml) heavy cream
½ cup (120ml) whole milk
5 large free-range egg yolks
⅓ cup (60g) superfine sugar,
 plus 2 tbsp to finish
few drops of vanilla extract

TIP If you do not have a blow torch, briefly place the ramekins under a very hot broiler to caramelize the sugar, but be careful not to overheat or the custard may melt.

Heat the oven to 275°F (140°C). Stand six ramekins or similar ovenproof dishes in a baking pan.

Melt the butter in a wide skillet. Add the rhubarb, honey, and seeds from the vanilla bean. Cook over high heat, tossing occasionally, for 5 to 6 minutes until the rhubarb is soft and slightly caramelized at the edges. Spoon into the ramekins.

Slowly heat the cream and milk together in a pan until just coming to a boil. Meanwhile, beat the egg yolks, sugar, and vanilla extract together in a bowl with a wooden spoon until evenly blended. Trickle the hot, creamy milk onto the egg mixture, beating constantly, until well combined. Strain the mixture through a strainer into a pitcher. Skim off any froth from the surface, then pour into the ramekins.

Pour warm water into the baking pan to come halfway up the sides of the ramekins. Bake for about 40 to 45 minutes until the custards are lightly set. To test, gently shake a ramekin—the custard should still be a little wobbly in the center. Remove the ramekins from the pan and let cool completely, then chill until ready to serve.

For the topping, sprinkle 1 tsp sugar evenly on top of each custard, then wave a cook's blow torch over the surface until the sugar has caramelized. Serve immediately.

MORE THAN
A QUARTER
OF PEOPLE
DO NOT FIND IT
EASY TO COOK
A MEAL THAT
THE WHOLE FAMILY
WILL EAT.

"Since when did everyone start getting so fussy? If children see you eating new dishes, then they might be prepared to try them. But my best advice is to get the kids to join in the cooking."

12 Malaysian curry

A typical Malaysian meal comprises a whole array of dishes and rarely begins with an appetizer. However, to keep the meal easy to prepare, I have focused on a fragrant curry with a couple of accompaniments and chosen to serve a light salad appetizer. The cool, delicate custard tart rounds off the spicy meal perfectly. This menu serves 6.

Arugula, fennel, watercress & pear salad
Malaysian chicken
    + Coconut rice
    + Stir-fried bok choy
Cardamom custard tart

planning your menu

THE DAY BEFORE...
• Make the curry paste and cook the curry, saving the green beans to add just before serving. Cool, cover, and chill.
• Make the pie dough for the tart, wrap, and place in the refrigerator

SEVERAL HOURS IN ADVANCE...
• Bake the pastry shell, prepare the filling, then bake the tart. Set aside to cool.

AN HOUR AHEAD...
• Take the curry out of the refrigerator. Prepare the green beans, ready to add.
• For the appetizer, prepare the fennel shavings and immerse in cold water. Wash the salad greens. Make the vinaigrette too.

HALF AN HOUR AHEAD...
• Reheat the curry in the oven at 350°F (180°C).
• Prepare the bok choy and have the flavoring ingredients ready.
• Cook the coconut rice.
• Drain the fennel and pat dry, toss with the salad greens.

JUST BEFORE SERVING...
• Assemble the salad appetizer and serve.
• Keep the curry warm and rest the rice while you eat the appetizer.
• Stir-fry the bok choy, fluff up the rice, and serve the main course.
• Cut the tart into neat slices and serve.

ARUGULA, FENNEL, WATERCRESS & PEAR SALAD

" This is a truly refreshing salad with added crunch from the fennel, a peppery kick from the arugula and watercress, and sweetness from the pears. A good choice to precede a curry, it would also make an ideal appetizer before rich meats like duck, game, or pork. The salad is lovely topped with a scattering of Parmesan shavings. "

6 servings

1 large fennel bulb, trimmed
1 large, ripe Comice or Bartlett pear
4oz (100g) watercress, stems removed
4oz (100g) wild arugula leaves

HONEY MUSTARD VINAIGRETTE:
1 tbsp wholegrain mustard
1 tbsp Dijon mustard
1 tbsp runny honey
1 tbsp lemon juice
  (or white wine vinegar)
4 tbsp extra virgin olive oil
sea salt and freshly ground black pepper

Cut the fennel into very thin slices, using a mandolin if possible. Plunge the fennel slices into a bowl of iced water and leave for 15 to 20 minutes to crisp up the leaves.

For the vinaigrette, combine all the ingredients in a screw-topped jar and shake to combine, seasoning to taste with salt and pepper. (Or whisk together in a bowl.) Set aside.

When ready to serve, drain the fennel, pat dry with a clean dish towel, and put into a large bowl. Quarter, core, and thinly slice the pear, then add to the bowl with the watercress and arugula. Drizzle over the vinaigrette, toss to combine, then pile the salad onto individual plates. Serve immediately.

MALAYSIAN CHICKEN

❝ For a laid-back Sunday lunch, serve up a curry and coconut rice—with or without a beer in hand. Curries generally improve in flavor the longer you let them stand, so make this the day before, leaving just the rice and vegetables to cook at the last minute. Traditionally, Malaysian chicken curry includes potatoes but I'm adding green beans instead—for color and a lighter meal. ❞

6 servings

CURRY PASTE:

5 garlic cloves, peeled and roughly chopped

4–5 long, red chiles, trimmed, seeded, and roughly chopped

3 lemon grass stalks, trimmed, outer leaves removed and thinly sliced

2-inch (5-cm) piece fresh gingerroot, peeled and chopped

4 large shallots, peeled and chopped

1 tsp ground turmeric

2–3 tbsp peanut oil

CURRY:

2¼lb (1kg) skinless and boneless chicken thighs

2 tbsp peanut oil

2 onions, peeled and thinly sliced

sea salt and freshly ground black pepper

4 kaffir lime leaves

1 cinnamon stick

3 star anise

1¾ cups (400ml) coconut milk

⅓ cup (100ml) Chicken stock (see page 246)

1 tsp palm sugar (or brown sugar)

2 tbsp light soy sauce

2 tbsp fish sauce

14oz (400g) green beans, trimmed and cut into 2-inch (5-cm) lengths

handful of cilantro leaves, roughly torn

First make the curry paste. Put the garlic, chiles, lemon grass, ginger, shallots, and turmeric in a food processor and whiz to a paste. With the motor running, trickle in the peanut oil and blend well, scraping the sides of the processor several times. (Or you can pound the ingredients together in batches using a mortar and pestle.)

To make the curry, cut the chicken into bite-size pieces. Heat the peanut oil in a large cast-iron casserole or heavy pan. Tip in the curry paste and stir over medium heat for a few minutes until fragrant. Add the onions and cook, stirring frequently, for 5 minutes until they are beginning to soften.

Season the chicken pieces with salt and pepper. Add to the pan and stir to coat them in the spice paste. Add the lime leaves, cinnamon stick, star anise, coconut milk, stock, sugar, soy and fish sauces, and bring to a boil. Reduce the heat to a simmer and cook gently for 30 to 40 minutes until the chicken is tender.

Skim off any excess oil on the surface of the curry. Taste and adjust the seasoning. Tip in the green beans, put the lid on, and cook for another 3 to 4 minutes until the beans are tender. Scatter the cilantro leaves over the curry and serve with coconut rice and stir-fried bok choy.

Coconut rice

Rinse the rice, drain, and tip into a heavy pan. Add the rest of the ingredients with ¾ cup (200ml) water, stir well, and bring to a boil, then reduce the heat to a simmer. Cover and gently simmer for 10 minutes. Take off the heat and let stand, still covered, for 5 to 10 minutes. Discard the ginger, fluff the rice with a fork, and serve while still hot.

6 servings

1¾ cups (350g) jasmine, Thai fragrant, or other long-grain rice

¾ cup (200ml) coconut milk

2-inch (5-cm) piece fresh gingerroot, peeled

pinch of sea salt

Stir-fried bok choy

6 servings

1⅓lb (600g) bok choy, washed

3 tbsp peanut oil

4 garlic cloves, peeled and thinly sliced

2 tbsp light soy sauce

2 tbsp oyster sauce

freshly ground black pepper

sesame oil, to drizzle

Separate the bok choy leaves and stems, then slice the stems on the diagonal. Heat the peanut oil in a large skillet or wok until hot. Add the garlic and sauté until it turns golden at the edges. Tip in the bok choy stems and stir-fry for a minute, then add the leaves together with the soy sauce, oyster sauce, and some black pepper. As soon as the leaves have wilted, transfer the vegetables to a warm plate and drizzle with a little sesame oil to serve.

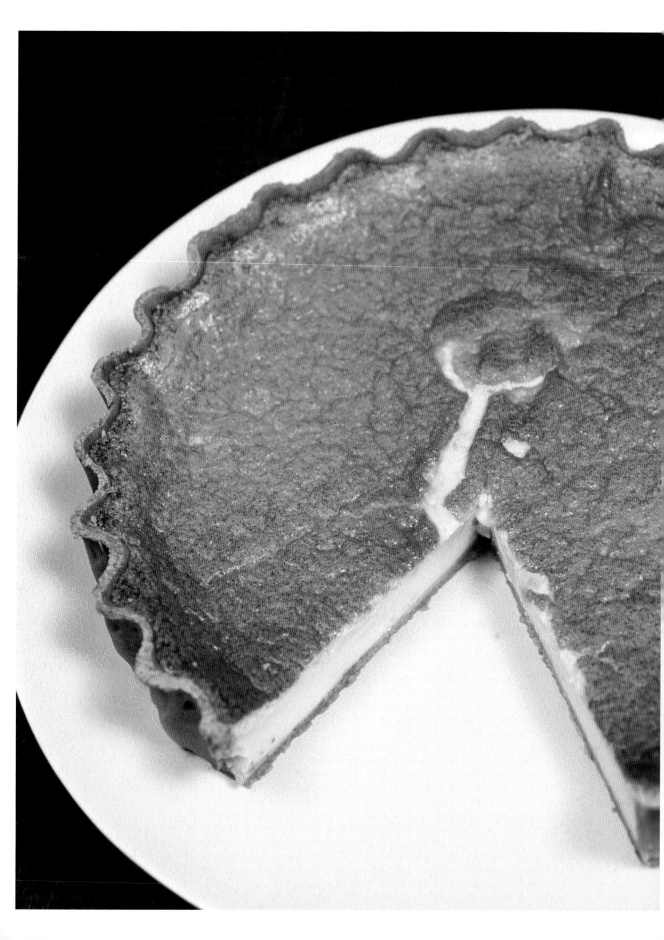

CARDAMOM CUSTARD TART

66 This delicious, light custard tart is infused with the subtle and warming flavors of cardamom and cinnamon. It is baked in a low oven until softly set—the custard filling will continue to firm up as it cools. 99

6–8 servings

10oz (300g) Sweet tart pie dough (see page 249)

flour, to dust

2½ cups (600ml) whole milk

8 cardamom pods, lightly crushed

1 cinnamon stick

½ cup (100g) superfine sugar

1½ tbsp cornstarch

4 eggs, separated

Roll out the pie dough thinly on a lightly floured surface and use to line a 9-inch (23-cm) fluted tart pan, about 2-inch (5-cm) deep, with a removable base. Leave the excess dough overhanging the sides. Press the dough well into the sides of the pan and pinch together or patch any gaps. Stand the tart pan on a baking sheet. Line the pastry shell with foil or baking parchment and dried beans and let rest in the refrigerator for 20 minutes. Meanwhile, heat the oven to 400°F (200°C).

For the filling, pour the milk into a pan and add the cardamom and cinnamon. Bring just to a boil, then remove from the heat and let stand for 15 minutes to allow the flavors to infuse.

Bake the pastry shell "blind" for 15 minutes, until the dough is just set. Remove the foil and beans, then return to the oven for 5 minutes to cook the base. Turn the oven down to 350°F (180°C).

In a large bowl, mix together the sugar, cornstarch, and egg yolks. Strain the milk through a fine strainer into a pitcher and discard the spices. Gradually stir the infused milk into the egg mixture. Whisk the egg whites until softly stiff and fold into the egg yolk mixture.

Pour the filling into the pastry shell. Bake for about 20 minutes until the filling is brown on top, then turn the oven down to 230°F (110°C) and bake for another 1 hour until the custard has just set. It should have a slight wobble in the center. Trim off the excess crust from the pastry and let cool completely before serving.

5 ways with...ONIONS

Stuffed onions
Serves 6

Heat the oven to 400°F (200°C). Peel and trim the root ends of 6 large onions, then slice off the top third to expose the layers. Blanch them in a pan of simmering salted water for 15 to 20 minutes until tender. Drain and refresh under cold running water. With a small spoon, scoop out the inner layers of each onion, leaving the outer two layers intact. Set aside the scooped-out onion flesh.

Sauté 2 finely chopped bacon slices with a little olive oil until golden brown and crisp Drain on paper towels. Whiz 4 slices of crustless white bread and a handful of Italian parsley in a food processor to fine crumbs. Take out 2–3 tbsp of the herbed bread crumbs and set aside. Add the reserved onion flesh to the processor and pulse gentl▼ to keep a coarse texture. Mix in the bacon and 2 tbsp Parmesan and season well. Toss another 2 tbsp Parmesan with the reserved bread crumbs.

Spoon the filling into the onions. Stand them on an oiled baking tray and sprinkle with the bread crumb mixture. Drizzle over a little olive oil and bake for 35 to 40 minutes c until the topping is golden and crisp. Serve with roast chicken, pork, or beef.

Braised leeks
Serves 4–6

Trim 6 large leeks and slice the white part into 2-inch (5-cm) lengths (saving the gree▼ parts for stock). Melt 2 tbsp butter in a heavy pan and add the leeks, salt, pepper, and 4 tbsp vegetable stock (or water). Bring the liquid to a low simmer and cover the pan with a lid. Braise for about 30 to 40 minutes until the leeks are tender. Transfer the leeks to a serving dish with a slotted spoon; keep warm. Boil the braising liquor to reduce and thicken, then pour over the leeks. Scatter over some chopped parsley and serve. Goes well with most fish and meat dishes.

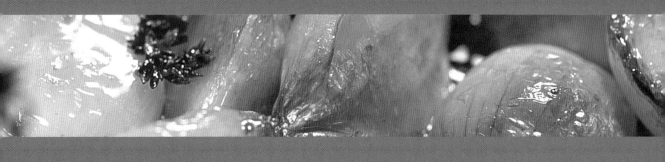

Caramelized shallots with thyme

Serves 4

Put 1lb (500g) shallots in a heavy pan with a little olive oil, a few thyme sprigs, some seasoning, and a splash of water. Cook the shallots for about 15 to 20 minutes until tender, then increase the heat to cook off the liquid and caramelize the shallots. Serve as a garnish to roast pork, beef, or poultry dishes.

Scallion & wild rice salad

Serves 4–6

Put 1lb (500g) cooked wild rice (or mixed leftover long-grain rice and wild rice) in a bowl. Add 1 minced red bell pepper, 1 minced red onion, 5–6 finely sliced scallions, and ⅓ cup toasted pine nuts or sliced almonds. Toss to mix. For the dressing, whisk together 1 tbsp Dijon mustard, 1 tbsp lemon juice, 1 tbsp runny honey, and 4 tbsp olive oil in a small bowl. Drizzle over the salad and toss to mix. Season to taste and serve at room temperature. A perfect side dish for a barbecue or a picnic.

Deep-fried onion rings

Serves 4

Peel 1 large Spanish onion and slice into rings. Season 2–3 tbsp all-purpose flour with salt and pepper, then toss the sliced onions in the flour to coat. Sift ½ cup self-rising flour into a bowl and make a well in the middle. Add 1 medium egg yolk and gradually beat in ⅔ cup (150ml) cold water to make a smooth batter. Whisk 2 medium egg whites in another bowl until softly peaking, then fold into the batter.

Heat enough peanut oil for deep-frying in a suitable pan to 350°F (180°C). (A bread cube dropped in should brown in 20 seconds.) Have a tray lined with paper towels ready. In batches, dip the onion rings in the batter and deep-fry for 3 to 4 minutes until golden and crisp. Drain on paper towels and sprinkle lightly with sea salt. Add a dusting of mild paprika if you wish, and serve immediately. A great accompaniment to steaks, sandwiches, or fried fish in batter.

13 Salmon in a package

This is easy to prepare, elegant, and full of enticing aromas as you cut into it! Instead of the foie gras appetizer—you could serve some little Parmesan puffs (see page 239) and olives with pre-lunch drinks. This menu serves 4–6.

Pan-seared foie gras with Puy lentils

Salmon en croûte
+ Minted hollandaise
+ Creamed leeks
+ Braised romaine lettuce

Roasted rhubarb crumble

planning your menu

A FEW DAYS AHEAD
• Order the foie gras from the butcher (arranging to collect it a day ahead, or fresh on the day if you can).

SEVERAL HOURS IN ADVANCE...
• For the main course, make the pie dough; wrap, and chill.
• Make the crumble topping. Sauté the rhubarb and let cool.

TWO HOURS IN ADVANCE...
• Prepare the spiced filling for the salmon, sandwich the fillets together, wrap in plastic wrap, and chill.
• Prepare the leeks and lettuce ready for cooking.

ABOUT AN HOUR AHEAD...
• Wrap the salmon in the dough; chill.
• Cook the lentils, dress with the vinaigrette; keep warm.
• Assemble the crumble. Prepare the flavored mascarpone.
• Put the salmon package into the oven 15 minutes before you start the meal. Bake the crumble at the same time in a second oven (or bake it before the salmon).
• Make the hollandaise; keep warm.

JUST BEFORE SERVING...
• Pan-fry the foie gras, plate the appetizer, and serve.
• Rest the salmon package while you cook the leeks and lettuce.
• Slice the salmon and serve the main course. Let the crumble stand, meanwhile.
• Serve the crumble with the mascarpone.

PAN-SEARED FOIE GRAS WITH PUY LENTILS

66 Foie gras may be the ultimate indulgence, but few people muster the courage to cook it. It's not difficult but you do need to handle the livers with care or it may prove to be an expensive disaster. Buy fresh foie gras from a good butcher and keep chilled as it deteriorates quickly. Foie gras also cooks quickly, so make sure the lentils are warm and ready to go before you sear it in a hot nonstick pan (without oil). 99

4–6 servings

1lb 2oz –1⅓lb (500–600g) foie gras,
   deveined and cut into 4 thick,
   even slices
sea salt and freshly ground black pepper

LENTILS:
1¼ cups (250g) Puy lentils, rinsed
   and drained
1 thyme sprig
1 bay leaf
1 garlic clove, peeled and crushed
4oz (100g) bacon trimmings
   (or 5 slices of unsmoked bacon)
1½ tbsp (20g) butter
1 carrot, peeled and finely diced
1 celery stalk, finely diced
1 leek, trimmed and finely diced
3oz (75g) bacon, cut into small dice
handful of chives, minced
3 tbsp olive oil
1 tbsp white wine vinegar

TIP The vegetables and bacon dice add a depth of flavor to the lentils, but you can omit them for a more straightforward dish.

First, cook the lentils.
Put them in a pan with the thyme, bay leaf, garlic, and bacon trimmings and add cold water to cover. Bring to a boil and cook for about 25 minutes until the lentils are tender. Remove the herbs and bacon, drain the lentils, and set aside.

Melt the butter
in another pan and add the carrot, celery, and leek. Sweat the vegetables for 10 minutes until softened, stirring frequently. In a nonstick pan, sauté the bacon dice until crispy. Add to the lentils along with the chives and vegetables.

Mix the olive oil
and wine vinegar together to make a vinaigrette and season with salt and pepper to taste. Pour two-thirds of the vinaigrette over the lentils, toss well, taste, and adjust the seasoning. Keep warm.

Heat a dry skillet
(preferably nonstick) until you can feel the heat rising from the pan. Quickly sauté each slice of foie gras until golden brown but soft in the center, seasoning as you cook. It should only take 1 to 2 minutes each side.

Slice the foie gras
in half horizontally. Pile the lentils onto warm plates and top with the foie gras. Drizzle the rest of the vinaigrette around the plates.

SALMON EN CROUTE

This dish is based on a classic recipe. Thick sides of salmon are sandwiched with currants and spiced butter, then encased in pie dough—here we're using basic pie dough as a change from the more typical puff pastry. Remember to let the salmon rest for a few minutes after baking before cutting.

4–6 servings

2 thick salmon fillets, about 1lb 2oz (500g) each, skinned

a little olive oil

4 tbsp (60g) unsalted butter, at room temperature

finely grated zest of 1 lemon

1 tbsp minced candied preserved ginger

½ cup (75g) currants

½ tsp freshly grated nutmeg

½ tsp ground cloves

sea salt and freshly ground black pepper

2¼lb (1kg) Basic pie dough (see page 249)

flour, to dust

2 egg yolks, beaten

few thyme sprigs

TIP To help keep the dough dry and crisp, you could wrap a layer of fine crêpes (see page 249) around the salmon before enclosing in the dough.

Check the salmon fillets for small pin bones, removing any that you find with tweezers. Line a baking tray with a lightly oiled piece of foil.

For the filling, mix the butter with the lemon zest, ginger, currants, and ground spices. Pat the salmon fillets dry with paper towels, then season lightly with salt and pepper. Spread the butter mix over one fillet, on the boned side, then sandwich the two salmon fillets together, in opposite directions so both ends are of an even thickness.

Roll out the pie dough thinly on a lightly floured surface to a rectangle, about ⅛ inch (3mm) thick. Put the salmon package in the center and brush the surrounding pastry with egg. Bring up the edges, trimming off any excess, and tuck them in before folding the rest of the dough over to form a neat package. Turn the whole thing over so that the seam is sitting on the bottom, and place on the prepared baking tray.

Brush the dough with the beaten egg. Lightly score the pastry to show 6–8 portions, then lightly score a herringbone or cross hatch pattern to decorate. Sprinkle with sea salt and pepper, and place the thyme sprigs on top. Chill for 15 minutes.

Heat the oven to 400°F (200°C). Bake the salmon for 20 to 25 minutes, depending on the thickness of the salmon. To test if ready, insert a skewer into the middle. It should feel warm for medium cooked salmon. A piping hot skewer indicates that the fish is well done.

Rest the salmon for 5 minutes, then slice thickly. Serve warm, with the minted hollandaise and accompaniments.

126

Minted hollandaise

3 tbsp white wine vinegar
½ tsp coriander seeds, finely crushed
5 egg yolks
¾ cup (175ml) light olive oil
2 tbsp mint leaves, finely shredded
Juice of ½ lemon
sea salt and freshly ground black pepper

Put the wine vinegar and crushed coriander seeds into a small pan. Boil until reduced by half. Place the egg yolks in a bain-marie (or a bowl set over a pan of barely simmering water). Immediately strain the vinegar through a strainer onto the yolks, whisking constantly until the mixture is pale, frothy, and doubled in volume. Remove the bowl from the heat and drizzle in the olive oil, whisking constantly. Add the mint, lemon juice, and season with salt and pepper. Cover and leave at room temperature until ready to serve.

Creamed leeks

Thinly slice the leeks. Heat the olive oil and butter in a skillet. Add the leeks and season with a touch of salt and the curry powder. Sweat over medium heat for 4 to 5 minutes until tender, stirring occasionally. Stir in the cream and heat through. Serve warm.

4–6 servings

3 leeks, trimmed
1 tbsp olive oil
1 tbsp (15g) butter
sea salt
1 tsp curry powder
⅔ cup (150ml) heavy cream

Braised romaine lettuce

4–6 servings

2–3 medium romaine lettuce, trimmed
a little olive oil, for cooking
sea salt and freshly ground black pepper
few thyme sprigs
1 tbsp butter
⅔ cup (150ml) vegetable stock

Slice the lettuce in half lengthwise. Heat the olive oil in a large skillet, add the lettuce, cut side down, and sauté for 1 to 2 minutes until lightly caramelized. Season with salt and pepper. Add the thyme and butter then pour in the stock. Bring to a simmer, cover, and gently braise for 4 to 5 minutes until the lettuce is tender. Lift the lettuce from the stock with a slotted spoon and serve immediately.

ROASTED RHUBARB CRUMBLE

" At the height of its early season, pink rhubarb is an intense pink color, which gives this crumble filling an enticing look. I sauté the rhubarb to enhance the flavor, add a bit of Japanese pickled ginger to give it warmth, and use vanilla-infused sugar to lend a sweet aroma. "

4–6 servings

1¾lb (800g) pink rhubarb, trimmed
¾ cup (150g) vanilla sugar (see tip)
few pieces of butter
¾ oz (20g) Japanese pickled ginger,
   minced

CRUMBLE TOPPING:

1 cup (150g) toasted, skinless hazelnuts
¾ cup (100g) all-purpose flour
4 tbsp (50g) unsalted butter, chilled and
   cut into small cubes
¼ cup (50g) raw brown sugar
pinch of freshly grated nutmeg
½ cup (40g) porridge oats

TO SERVE:

finely grated zest of ½ lemon
¾ cup (200g) mascarpone

TIP To make your own vanilla sugar, simply stick 3 vanilla beans into a 1lb (500g) jar of superfine sugar and leave for a few days to let the flavor infuse. Vanilla beans that have been used (ie had their seeds extracted) are fine for this; indeed it is a good way to make full use of expensive vanilla beans.

Heat the oven to 375°F (190°C). Cut the rhubarb stalks into 1½–2-inch (4–5-cm) lengths. Wash if necessary and pat dry in a clean dish towel.

Toss the rhubarb in the vanilla sugar. Heat a heavy sauté pan, then tip in the fruit and add 2 tbsp water. Add a few pieces of butter to enrich the flavor and let cook for a couple of minutes. Turn the rhubarb using a thin metal spoon or spatula so the fruit stays intact as far as possible; it should not become too pulpy. Continue cooking for another 3 to 5 minutes until the pieces feel just tender when pierced with the tip of a knife. Stir in the ginger, remove from the heat, and let cool.

Meanwhile, make the crumble. Put the hazelnuts into a large bowl and lightly crush with the end of a rolling pin. With the tips of your fingers, rub the flour and butter together in another bowl until they form a crumb-like mixture. Tip in the raw brown sugar, grated nutmeg, oats, and hazelnuts. Mix well.

Lay the fruit in a baking dish, then scatter the crumble topping evenly over the top. Bake for 20 to 25 minutes until the topping is nicely browned. Let stand for about 10 minutes. Meanwhile, mix the lemon zest into the mascarpone. Serve the rhubarb crumble warm, with a dollop of the flavored mascarpone.

14 Surf 'n' turf

Full of zesty flavors, this is a vibrant, colorful menu. A tangy tomato dressing enlivens pan-fried steaks and a tangy mango salsa complements fresh crabmeat. For a more straightforward appetizer, simply serve the crab mix on chicory leaves with lime wedges on the side, omitting the salsa. This menu serves 6.

Crab wraps with mango salsa
Sirloin steak with tomato tarragon dressing
+ Oven fries
Lemon tart

planning your menu

THE DAY BEFORE...
• Make the pie dough for the tart, wrap in plastic wrap, and refrigerate.

SEVERAL HOURS IN ADVANCE...
• Prepare the crab mix, lettuce, and salsa for the appetizer, but don't add the mango or mint at this stage.
• Make the lemon tart, bake, and set aside to cool.
• Make the tomato dressing for the steak, but don't add the herbs.

TWO HOURS AHEAD...
• Take the steaks out of the refrigerator.
• Peel the potatoes, cut the fries, and blanch them, then refresh, drain well, and toss in oil to coat.

TWENTY MINUTES AHEAD...
• Bake the fries.
• Make the crab wraps.

JUST BEFORE SERVING...
• Toss the mango and mint into the salsa and assemble the appetizer.
• Add the herbs to the tomato and tarragon dressing.
• Pan-fry the steaks and rest while you eat the appetizer (or afterward if you prefer).
• Slice the steaks and serve with the dressing and fries.
• Dust the tart with confectioners' sugar and slice to serve.

CRAB WRAPS WITH MANGO SALSA

"Sweet, crunchy Iceberg lettuce leaves are the 'wraps' for this refreshing, zingy appetizer. All the components—the crab filling, lettuce leaves, and salsa ingredients—can be prepared in advance, to be assembled easily just before serving. To keep the mango fresh and vibrant, however, I suggest you add it to the other salsa ingredients with the mint—at the last minute."

6 servings

10oz (300g) white crabmeat
½ red chile seeded and very finely diced
1 shallot, peeled and very finely diced
small handful of cilantro, leaves chopped
1 tbsp wholegrain mustard
6–7 tbsp Mayonnaise (see page 247)
sea salt and freshly ground black pepper
squeeze of lime juice
1 large head of Iceberg lettuce, washed

SALSA:
1 red chile, seeded and very finely diced
1 small red onion, peeled and very finely diced
juice of 1 lime
1 tbsp sesame oil
1 tbsp olive oil, plus extra to drizzle
2 large ripe mangoes, peeled and cubed
handful of mint leaves, shredded

Put the crabmeat into a bowl and run your fingers through the meat to pick out any little bits of shell. Add the chile, shallot, and cilantro and fork through to mix. Stir the mustard into the mayonnaise, then mix enough into the crabmeat to bind the mixture. Season with salt and pepper and add lime juice to taste.

For the salsa, combine all the ingredients except the mangoes and mint in a bowl. Season lightly with salt and pepper.

Separate the lettuce into leaves, then trim the sides to give 4–4½ inch (10–12cm) wide strips. Carefully flatten the trimmed lettuce leaves on a cutting board, without tearing them. Place a heaping tablespoonful of crab filling along one end of each strip and roll the lettuce leaf around the filling to encase it. Place, seam side down, on a plate. Continue until you've used all the crab filling.

When ready to serve, stir the chopped mangoes and shredded mint into the salsa and spoon onto a serving plate. Arrange the crab wraps on top. Drizzle a little olive oil over the wraps and sprinkle with sea salt and pepper. Serve immediately.

133

SIRLOIN STEAK WITH TOMATO TARRAGON DRESSING

" This is a healthier version of steak and fries, with the traditional béarnaise sauce replaced by a tomato tarragon dressing and lower fat oven fries. The dressing is one of my favorite sauces to serve with steak. It is so quick and easy—the ingredients are simply thrown together. Start cooking the steaks 10 minutes before the fries will be ready. "

6 servings

olive oil, for cooking
6 sirloin steaks, 7–9oz (200–250g) each
sea salt and freshly ground black pepper
few pieces of butter

TOMATO TARRAGON DRESSING:
6 medium tomatoes
5 tbsp tomato ketchup
2 tbsp Worcestershire sauce
1–2 tbsp Dijon (or wholegrain) mustard
few dashes of Tabasco
juice of 1 lemon
2 tbsp balsamic vinegar
2 tbsp olive oil
2 large shallots, peeled and chopped
large handful of tarragon, leaves chopped
handful of parsley, leaves chopped

First, make the dressing. Halve the
tomatoes, squeeze out the seeds, then mince the flesh and place in a bowl. Add the rest of the ingredients, except the herbs, and season with salt and pepper to taste. Set aside.

Heat a skillet with a little olive oil until hot. Season the
steaks with salt and pepper. Sear them in the hot skillet in batches for 1 to 1½ minutes on each side, depending on thickness. Add a few pieces of butter to the skillet during cooking and spoon the melted butter over the steaks to baste them. When ready, they will feel springy if lightly pressed.

Transfer the steaks to a warm plate, lightly cover
with foil, and let rest in a warm place for 5 to 10 minutes. Meanwhile, stir the chopped tarragon and parsley into the tomato dressing.

Slice the steaks thickly on the diagonal, arrange on
warm plates and spoon over the tomato tarragon dressing. Serve with the hot oven fries on the side.

Oven fries

Heat the oven to 400°F (200°C). Peel the potatoes and cut into
½-inch (1-cm) thick sticks. Blanch in a pan of boiling salted water for 3 minutes. Drain well and pat dry with a clean dish towel. Spread the fries out on an oiled baking tray. Drizzle with oil, season generously with salt, and scatter over the rosemary. Cook in the oven for about 30 to 40 minutes until golden brown and crisp, turning the potatoes several times during cooking to ensure even coloring.

6 servings

2¼lb (1kg) large round red potatoes
sea salt
peanut oil, to oil and drizzle
few rosemary sprigs, leaves only

134

LEMON TART

> A good lemon tart was once the hallmark of a great pastry chef and the tart featured on the menus of all fine restaurants. The secret is to bake the tart in a very low oven to prevent the lemon custard filling from bubbling and cracking as it sets. The custard will firm up as it cools.

6–8 servings

10oz (300g) Sweet pie dough (see page 249)
flour, to dust
2 large eggs
4 large egg yolks
scant 1 cup (180g) superfine sugar
²⁄₃ cup (200ml) heavy cream
juice of 2 lemons
confectioners' sugar, to dust
crème fraîche, to serve

TIP For a professional finish, run a cook's blow torch over the surface to caramelize the confectioners' sugar and give the tart a "crème brûlée" effect, as illustrated.

Roll out the pie dough
on a lightly floured surface and use to line an 8-inch (20-cm) tart pan with a removable base. Leave the excess dough overhanging the sides. Rest in the refrigerator for 20 minutes.

Heat the oven
to 375°F (190°C). Line the dough with foil or baking parchment and fill with dried beans. Bake "blind" for 15 minutes—the sides should just begin to color. Remove the beans and foil, then bake for another 5 minutes until the pastry base is cooked and lightly golden. Lower the oven setting to 230°F (110°C).

Whisk the eggs,
egg yolks, and sugar together in a bowl, then stir in the cream. Finally add the lemon juice (this will thicken the cream). Strain the lemon filling through a fine strainer into a large pitcher.

Pour half the filling
into the pastry shell. Place the pan on the bottom shelf of the oven. Pull out the shelf halfway, keeping the pan level, and pour in the remaining lemon filling. Carefully push the shelf back into the oven and bake for 50 to 60 minutes until the filling is almost set. It should have a slight wobble in the center. Carefully trim the pastry level to the top of the pan and let cool completely.

Dust the tart
liberally with confectioners' sugar. Cut neat slices with a warm knife and serve on its own or with some crème fraîche.

NEARLY HALF OF ALL FAMILIES NEVER SIT DOWN FOR A DAILY MEAL TOGETHER.

" It's what the dining room table was invented for ...eating together as a family is really important to me and I am determined to get families back around the table together. **"**

15 Italian essence

I love the simplicity of this menu—chicken braised in Marsala with pan-fried chicory, a creamy saffron-scented soup, and an easy, prepare-ahead dessert to finish. It works equally well as a hassle-free Sunday lunch or smart supper. This menu serves 4.

Saffron & cauliflower soup

Chicken Marsala with red chicory

Coffee & chocolate mousse cups

planning your menu

THE DAY BEFORE...
• Prepare the mousse cups and chill.

TWO HOURS IN ADVANCE...
• Joint the chicken and bring to room temperature.

FROM AN HOUR AHEAD...
• Make the soup, saving the garnish to prepare at the last moment.
• Trim and separate the chicory, ready to cook.

ABOUT 15 MINUTES AHEAD...
• Prepare the garnish for the soup.
• Sauté the chicken and add the Marsala.

JUST BEFORE SERVING...
• Gently reheat the soup and serve with the cauliflower garnish.
• Let the chicken braise while you have the appetizer.
• Sauté the chicory and serve the main course.
• Top the mousses with cream, decorate, and serve.

SAFFRON & CAULIFLOWER SOUP

"Cooking cauliflower in a poaching liquid of chicken stock and milk helps to keep it pale and velvety, while saffron delicately enhances its flavor. The island of Sardinia is renowned for its saffron and the spice features in Italian cooking."

4 servings

2 cups (500ml) Chicken (or vegetable)
  stock (see page 246)
2 cups (500ml) milk
2 pinches of saffron strands
sea salt and freshly ground black pepper
1 large cauliflower, cut into florets
2 tbsp (25g) butter
2 tbsp chopped parsley
olive oil, to drizzle

Pour the stock and milk into a large pan and add a pinch of saffron and a generous pinch of salt. Bring to a boil, add the cauliflower florets, and lower the heat to a simmer. Cook for about 5 to 8 minutes until the cauliflower is just tender when pierced with a skewer.

Using a slotted spoon, take out one-quarter of the cauliflower florets and set aside. Put the rest into a blender, add enough of the poaching liquid to half-fill the blender, and whiz to a very smooth purée. (Do this in two batches if you need to.)

Return the purée to the pan and add enough of the remaining poaching liquid to obtain a soup consistency. Add another pinch of saffron and reheat gently, seasoning to taste with salt and pepper. Stir in more liquid if the soup is too thick.

Melt the butter in a pan until it begins to foam, then add the reserved cauliflower and sauté for a few minutes until golden brown. Toss in half the chopped parsley and cook until crisp.

Place the cauliflower florets and parsley in the center of four soup bowls, then pour in the soup, to one side. Serve immediately, topped with a drizzle of olive oil, a sprinkling of parsley, and a grinding of black pepper.

CHICKEN MARSALA WITH RED CHICORY

" An old Italian favorite, traditionally chicken breasts (or veal scallops) are pounded into thin scallops, dredged in seasoned flour, browned, and then cooked with Marsala wine. I prefer to brown the chicken pieces whole, to keep them juicy and succulent, and then braise them with a generous amount of Marsala. "

4 servings

olive oil, for cooking
few thyme sprigs
½ head of garlic (unpeeled), cut
   horizontally
1 large chicken, jointed into 8 pieces
sea salt and freshly ground black pepper
½ bottle of Marsala (375ml)
handful of Italian parsley, leaves roughly
   chopped

PAN-FRIED RED CHICORY:
4 heads of red chicory, trimmed
olive oil, for cooking
sea salt and freshly ground black pepper

Heat a thin film of olive oil

in a wide skillet. Add the thyme and garlic and cook gently for a minute. Season the chicken pieces with salt and pepper and add them to the skillet, skin side down. Sauté for 4 to 5 minutes until golden brown, then turn the chicken pieces over and cook on the other side for 3 to 4 minutes. (You may need to brown the chicken in batches if your pan is not wide enough.)

Pour in the Marsala

and stand well back as it may flambé. Lower the heat and braise the chicken for 10 to 15 minutes until cooked through. To test, pierce the thickest part of a chicken thigh and press lightly—the juices should run clear.

Separate the chicory

into individual leaves. Heat a skillet with a thin layer of olive oil. Add the chicory leaves, season with a little salt and pepper, and toss over high heat for 1 to 2 minutes to slightly wilt the leaves. They should still have a slight bite to them.

Pile the chicken

onto a large platter and arrange the sautéed chicory leaves around. Spoon over the Marsala sauce and serve immediately, with a sprinkling of chopped parsley.

COFFEE & CHOCOLATE MOUSSE CUPS

" This is a delicious, no-bake mocha dessert that uses mascarpone rather than eggs as a base for the mousse. Do make the espresso strong—the coffee flavor needs to hold up against the chocolate. If you don't have an espresso maker, get a double espresso takeout from your nearest coffee shop! "

4 servings

4oz (100g) good-quality semisweet chocolate (about 60–65% cocoa solids)
½ cup (125g) mascarpone
2 tbsp confectioners' sugar
4 tbsp strong espresso coffee, cooled
⅔ cup (150ml) heavy cream

TO FINISH:
4 tbsp heavy cream
a little semisweet grated chocolate
few amaretti cookies, crushed

TIP To melt the chocolate in a microwave, break into small pieces and tip into a bowl. Microwave on high for a minute, give the pieces a stir, then microwave again for another minute. Stir the chocolate until smooth. This method is only suitable for semisweet or bittersweet chocolate. White chocolate, in particular, is likely to seize as it overheats in the microwave.

Break the chocolate into small pieces and melt in a heatproof bowl set over a pan of barely simmering water. Stir until smooth, then remove the bowl from the heat and let cool.

With a hand whisk, beat the mascarpone and confectioners' sugar together until smooth, then whisk in the espresso and the melted chocolate.

In another bowl, whip the heavy cream until soft peaks form. Fold the cream into the mocha mixture until well combined. Spoon the mousse into four cappuccino cups or ramekins and chill overnight.

Just before serving, lightly whip the 4 tbsp heavy cream until thick and swirl over the mousses. Sprinkle the grated chocolate and crushed amaretti on top and serve immediately.

16 Wild food

This menu brings together some of the great flavors of fall—wild mushrooms, game, figs, and almonds. For a lighter, faster appetizer, you could omit the pasta and simply pile the mushrooms onto warm toasted baguette slices to serve as bruschetta. This menu serves 4.

Tagliatelle of wild mushrooms
Venison with red wine & chocolate sauce
+ Creamed cabbage & celeriac with pancetta
+ Gratin dauphinoise

Fig & frangipane tart

planning your menu

A DAY IN ADVANCE...
• Make the pasta and keep well wrapped in the refrigerator.

ABOUT TWO HOURS AHEAD...
• Cut the tagliatelle and keep covered, ready to cook later.
• Take the venison out of the refrigerator to bring to room temperature.
• Make the sauce for the venison, but don't add the vinegar or chocolate yet.
• Prepare the gratin dauphinoise.
• For the appetizer, prepare the mushrooms and flavoring ingredients, ready to cook.
• Make the frangipane for the tarts.

AN HOUR IN ADVANCE...
• Shape the pastry disks, place on a baking sheet, and chill.
• Shred the cabbage and immerse in cold water. Sweat the root vegetables; set aside.
• Bake the potatoes dauphinoise.
• Prepare the figs and assemble the tarts ready to bake.

JUST BEFORE SERVING...
• Cook the pasta and mushrooms.
• Sear the venison and put in the oven to finish cooking while you have the appetizer.
• Drain the cabbage.
• Rest the venison.
• Put the fig tarts into the oven to bake.
• Finish the sauce and cabbage, plate the main course, and serve.
• Glaze the tarts and let stand for 5 minutes before serving.

TAGLIATELLE OF WILD MUSHROOMS

"Fresh pasta soaks up the lovely, earthy flavors of wild mushrooms to delicious effect. When they're not in season, use crimini mushrooms and a good handful of dried cèpes. Soak the dried mushrooms in the usual way, reducing the soaking liquid with a touch of cream to create a flavorful sauce for the pasta."

4 servings

PASTA:
scant 2 cups (275g) Italian "00" flour or strong flour, plus extra to dust
pinch of fine sea salt
2 whole eggs
3 egg yolks
1 tbsp olive oil

MUSHROOMS:
1–1¼lb (500g) mixed wild mushrooms (such as cèpes, girolles, trompettes, mousserons), cleaned and trimmed
2 shallots, peeled and minced
1 garlic clove, peeled and crushed
1–2 tbsp olive oil, plus extra to drizzle
sea salt and freshly ground black pepper
few Italian parsley sprigs, chopped
small handful of chives, chopped
handful of arugula leaves

TO SERVE:
Parmesan shavings

To make the pasta
put the ingredients into a food processor and whiz until the mixture resembles coarse crumbs. Tip into a bowl and knead together to form a dough. Turn onto a lightly floured surface and knead for a few minutes until the dough is smooth and elastic. Wrap in plastic wrap and rest for at least half an hour.

Cut the dough
into two pieces and work with one at a time, keeping the other piece covered with plastic wrap. Roll out the dough thinly and feed through the pasta machine on its widest setting several times. Now adjust the setting by one notch each time you pass the pasta through, gradually rolling out the pasta more thinly until it is about $\frac{1}{32}$ inch (1mm) thick. Hang the pasta to dry over the back of a clean chair while you roll the rest of the dough.

Pass the pasta sheets
through the machine with the tagliatelle cutters fitted or cut them by hand—the tagliatelle should be about $\frac{1}{2}$ inch (1cm) wide. Lift the noodles from one end, dust lightly with flour to prevent them sticking, and twirl them into a nest on a tray. Repeat with the rest of the pasta.

Halve or slice
larger mushrooms; leave small ones whole. In a pan, sauté the shallots and garlic in olive oil until lightly browned, then add the mushrooms and cook for a few minutes. Season and add the parsley, chives, and arugula toward the end.

Cook the tagliatelle
in boiling salted water for 1½ to 2 minutes until *al dente*. Drain the pasta and toss quickly with a little olive oil in a hot pan. Tip the mushroom mixture on top and toss well. Season again and add a little more olive oil if necessary. Serve topped with fresh Parmesan shavings.

VENISON WITH RED WINE & CHOCOLATE SAUCE

" Venison is a sumptuous, lean red meat with little saturated fat and cholesterol—great for anyone keeping an eye on calories. It is not uncommon to pair venison with red wine and chocolate—a little grated chocolate whisked into the red wine sauce helps to thicken and enrich it. Do use good quality brown stock—ideally homemade—you won't get the correct consistency for the sauce if you resort to stock cubes. "

4 servings

5oz (150g) smoked bacon, cut into small
   cubes
9oz (250g) shallots (about 4 large ones),
   peeled and roughly chopped
few thyme sprigs
2 bay leaves
1 tsp black peppercorns, crushed
olive oil, for cooking
1½ cups (350ml) red wine
4 cups (1 liter) brown Chicken stock
   (see page 246)
sea salt and freshly ground black pepper
4 venison fillets, about 5oz (150g) each,
   trimmed
1 tsp raspberry vinegar
¾oz (20g) bittersweet chocolate, grated

Sauté the bacon and shallots with the herbs and crushed peppercorns in a little olive oil, using a wide pan, for about 6 to 8 minutes until the shallots have softened. Add the red wine and boil for 10 minutes until reduced by half. Add the chicken stock and keep boiling until reduced to a syrupy consistency. This may take up to 20 to 25 minutes. Pass through a strainer into a clean pan, taste, and adjust the seasoning.

Heat the oven to 425°F (220°C). Heat an ovenproof skillet on the stove and add a little olive oil. Season the venison fillets and brown them in the hot skillet, allowing 3 to 4 minutes each side. Remove the pan from the heat and wrap the venison with foil to help retain the moisture. Put the skillet into the oven and cook for 6 to 8 minutes, turning the fillets halfway through. Let rest in a warm place for 5 minutes or so.

While the meat rests, add the raspberry vinegar to the sauce and reheat gently. Take the pan off the heat and whisk in the grated chocolate until it melts and the sauce is smooth. (If it turns grainy, just pass through a fine strainer and it should become smooth again.) Taste and adjust the seasoning.

Slice the venison and arrange on warm plates. Pour the sauce around and serve immediately, with the accompaniments.

152

Creamed cabbage & celeriac with pancetta

Heat a little olive oil in a large, wide pan and sauté the chopped bacon until golden brown. Add the carrots and celeriac and sweat the vegetables for 6 to 8 minutes until softened. Add the butter and stir the cabbage through. Cook for 3 to 4 minutes until the cabbage is tender. Pour in the cream and simmer to reduce slightly. Season generously with salt and pepper and serve.

4 servings

olive oil, for cooking
4oz (100g) lean bacon (about 8 slices), chopped
14oz (400g) carrots (2–3 large ones), peeled and diced
½ celeriac, peeled and diced
4 tbsp (50g) unsalted butter
1 small savoy cabbage, trimmed and finely shredded
¾ cup (200ml) heavy cream
sea salt and freshly ground black pepper

Gratin dauphinoise

4–6 servings

a little olive oil, to drizzle
¾ cup (200ml) whole milk
¾ cup (200ml) heavy cream
1 bay leaf
1 garlic clove, peeled and smashed
2¼lb (1 kg) waxy potatoes, such as round red or Charlotte
7oz (200g) medium Cheddar, grated
sea salt and freshly ground black pepper

Heat the oven to 400°F (200°C). Lightly oil a deep gratin dish. Put the milk, cream, bay leaf, and garlic in a pan and heat until simmering. When the liquid begins to bubble up the sides of the pan, turn off the heat and let cool slightly.

Peel and finely slice the potatoes, using a mandolin. Scatter one-third of the cheese over the bottom of a baking dish and cover with a layer of the potato slices, overlapping them slightly. Season generously with salt and pepper. Continue layering until you've used up all the cheese and potatoes, seasoning the layers and finishing with cheese. Strain the creamy milk, discarding the bay leaf and garlic. Pour over the potatoes to come two-thirds up the sides (you may not need all of it). Gently press the potatoes down to help them absorb the liquid. Sprinkle with a little more cheese and bake for 35 to 40 minutes or until the potatoes are golden brown and tender when prodded with a sharp knife. Let stand for a few minutes before serving.

FIG & FRANGIPANE TART

" These beautiful individual tarts make the most of that classic Mediterranean combination of honeyed figs and almonds. For a sumptuous finish, serve them with mascarpone laced with a splash of amaretto or sweet dessert wine. "

Makes 4–6

1lb (500g) ready-made puff pastry
flour, to dust
1 egg yolk, beaten, to glaze
10–12 ripe figs

FRANGIPANE:
1 stick (100g) butter, softened to room
   temperature
1 cup (100g) confectioners' sugar, plus
   extra to dust
1 large egg, beaten
generous 1 cup (100g) ground almonds
⅛ cup (25g) all-purpose flour

TO SERVE:
runny honey, to drizzle
heavy cream, to serve

TIP If you can only find unripe figs in your local supermarket, leave them in the fruit bowl next to a bunch of bananas to encourage the ripening process.

First make the frangipane. Cream the butter and confectioners' sugar together in a bowl, then slowly add the egg, mixing until it is fully incorporated. Add the ground almonds and flour and fold through until evenly combined. Let the mixture rest for about 5 minutes. Heat the oven to 400°F (200°C).

Roll out the puff pastry thinly on a lightly floured surface until about ⅛ inch (3mm) thick. Using a small plate or saucer as a guide, cut out 4–6 circles from the pastry. Score a ½-inch (1-cm) border around the edge of each circle, making sure you don't cut right through the pastry. Lift the circles onto a large baking tray and glaze the border with the egg yolk. Smooth a thin layer of frangipane over the center of each pastry circle.

Slice two figs horizontally into circles. Cut the rest of the figs into wedges. Arrange on top of the frangipane like a flower, with a fig circle in the center surrounded by fig wedges. Dust with a little confectioners' sugar and bake until the pastry is crisp and golden, about 20 minutes. The pastry border will puff up around the fig flowers.

While still warm, drizzle honey over the figs and frangipane to glaze. Cool slightly before serving, with cream.

"Fish is one of the most delicious and nutritious foods available to us. Fish suppliers, sadly, are now few and far between, but if you've got one near you, treasure him. Always check fish and shellfish carefully for quality and freshness before you buy. Remember, fish is such an easy thing to cook that it's perfect for a hassle-free meal."

17 Fast food

An effortless meal that needs little planning or advance preparation. To make it even more straightforward, you could omit the appetizer and instead serve an antipasti spread of Italian cured meats, tomatoes, olives, and artichoke hearts. This menu serves 4

Baby squid in tomato sauce with chard
Griddled spring chicken & vegetables on focaccia
Iced berries with white chocolate sauce

planning your menu

SEVERAL HOURS (OR A DAY) AHEAD...
• Put the chicken to marinate.
• Freeze the berries.

TWO HOURS IN ADVANCE...
• Prepare the ingredients for the appetizer, ready to cook.

30 MINUTES AHEAD...
• Make the white chocolate sauce and keep warm.
• Braise the squid and blanch the chard for the appetizer; refresh in cold water.

JUST BEFORE SERVING...
• Cook the chicken, vegetables, and focaccia on the griddle; keep warm in a low oven.
• Sauté the chard, assemble the appetizer, and serve.
• Plate the main course, add the dressing, and serve.
• Divide the frozen berries among plates and pour the warm chocolate sauce over as you serve.

BABY SQUID IN TOMATO SAUCE WITH CHARD

" An Italian friend who grew up in Tuscany described this rustic dish to me and I was fascinated by the clever pairing of fish with Swiss chard. The tender braised squid really benefits from the succulent chard leaves and the flavors are held together with white wine, garlic, and chile. This dish would also make a delicious light meal, served with a rustic Italian loaf or some pasta. "

4 servings

2–3 tbsp olive oil
1 shallot, peeled and minced
1 celery stalk, trimmed and finely
    chopped
1 leek, trimmed and finely chopped
3 garlic cloves, peeled and minced
1–1¼lb (500g) baby squid, cleaned and
    cut into rings
sea salt and freshly ground black pepper
⅓ cup (100ml) dry white wine
4 ripe plum tomatoes, quartered

SAUTÉED CHARD:

1 large Swiss chard, about 1½lb
    (750g), washed and trimmed
2–3 tbsp olive oil
2 garlic cloves, peeled and chopped
½ red chile, seeded and chopped

Heat the olive oil in a large heavy pan and add the shallot, celery, leek, and garlic. Stir over medium heat for 6 to 8 minutes until the vegetables are soft and translucent.

Add the squid and season well with salt and pepper. Cook for a few minutes, then pour in the white wine. Lower the heat and gently braise the squid for about 10 to 15 minutes until tender. Tip in the quartered tomatoes and cook over medium heat for another 5 minutes. Keep warm.

Coarsely chop the Swiss chard in the meantime, separating the stems and leaves into two piles. Heat the olive oil in a large pan and gently sauté the garlic and chile until the garlic turns golden. Meanwhile, blanch the chard stems in a pan of boiling salted water for 4 to 5 minutes, then add the leaves and cook for another minute. Drain well. Add the chard to the garlic and chile and toss over medium heat for a few minutes until the stems are tender. Season generously with salt and pepper.

As soon as it's ready, divide the chard among warm plates, add the braised squid, and serve.

GRIDDLED SPRING CHICKEN & VEGETABLES ON FOCACCIA

"This is quick and easy to cook on the griddle and when the weather turns warm you can take it outside to barbecue. If you have time, marinate the chicken pieces in the olive oil overnight to allow the flavors of the garlic and rosemary to infuse."

4 servings

2 spring chickens or squab chickens, about 1lb (450g) each
few rosemary sprigs, leaves only
3–4 garlic cloves, halved, with skin on
olive oil, to drizzle
sea salt and freshly ground black pepper
2 large zucchini, trimmed
1 small eggplant, trimmed
1 large yellow bell pepper
1 large red bell pepper
few thyme sprigs
1 large (or 2 medium) focaccia loaves

BALSAMIC DRESSING:
6 tbsp olive oil
3 tbsp balsamic vinegar

TIP If you are cooking this dish for a larger crowd, I suggest you poach the chicken pieces for about 10 minutes in advance. This reduces the time needed for griddling and makes it easier to ensure all the chicken is cooked through.

Carve out the chicken
breasts and legs (or get your butcher to do this). Put them into a large bowl with the rosemary and 2 garlic cloves. Drizzle generously with olive oil and season well with pepper. Set aside to marinate.

Cut the zucchini
into ½-inch (1-cm) thick circles. Slice the eggplant into circles of a similar thickness. Halve, core, and seed the bell peppers, then cut into wedges. Place the vegetables in a bowl, add the remaining garlic and thyme, and toss with a generous drizzle of olive oil. Season with salt and pepper.

For the dressing,
mix the olive oil and balsamic vinegar together and season with salt and pepper to taste. Set aside.

Heat a griddle pan
until almost smoking. Using tongs, place the vegetables on the griddle and cook for 6 to 8 minutes, turning them halfway through cooking. Remove to a plate and set aside.

Season the chicken
with salt and cook on the griddle, allowing about 3 to 4 minutes each side for the breasts, 5 to 6 minutes each side for the legs. Check it is cooked through—the meat will be firm and the juices should run clear when the thickest part is pierced with a skewer. Transfer to a plate and keep warm.

Cut the focaccia
into four 4–4½-inch (10–12-cm) squares. If very thick, slice them in half horizontally. Griddle for 20 seconds on each side to warm through—watch closely as they burn easily. Brush with a little olive oil if you wish and place on warm plates.

Spoon the griddled veg
onto the bread and top each serving with a chicken breast and leg. Spoon over the balsamic dressing and serve immediately.

ICED BERRIES WITH WHITE CHOCOLATE SAUCE

" This must be the easiest dessert to prepare. Simply freeze a selection of berries overnight and pour over some melted white chocolate to serve. The berries will start to thaw as soon as they come in contact with the warm chocolate sauce. "

4 servings

generous ¾ cup (125g) blueberries
1 cup (125g) raspberries
generous ¾ cup (125g) blackberries
1⅛ cups (125g) red currants
generous ¾ cup (125g) strawberries, hulled and quartered
7oz (200g) white chocolate

TIP It is important to cut any larger berries, such as strawberries, into even-size pieces to ensure that all the fruit defrosts at the same rate when you pour the sauce on.

Arrange the fruit in a shallow freezer container or on a baking tray and freeze for at least 2 hours or overnight until solid.

Break the chocolate into small pieces and place in a bowl set over a pan of barely simmering water, making sure the bowl isn't in direct contact with the water. Allow the chocolate to melt slowly, stirring occasionally, until smooth. Pour the melted chocolate into a warm small serving pitcher. If not serving immediately, keep the chocolate sauce warm by sitting the pitcher in a pan of hot water.

Divide the frozen berries among four chilled serving plates. Drizzle the warm chocolate sauce over the fruit at the table.

MORE THAN HALF OF ALL HOUSEHOLDS WATCH THE TV WHEN EATING TOGETHER.

"Switch the television off at mealtimes. You don't need that going on when you're trying to talk to your friends and family. Mealtimes are about savoring the food on your plate, appreciating it, and taking your time over it. You don't need any extras with that."

18 Quick & easy

I love the rustic flavors here, especially the combination of tastes and textures in the salad and the peasant-style main dish. The entire three-course meal can be rustled up in next to no time—Sunday lunch has never been easier! This menu serves 4.

Vine tomato & bread salad

Italian sausages with lentils

Lemon posset

planning your menu

THE DAY BEFORE...
• Make the dessert and refrigerate (or prepare on the day at least 3 hours ahead).

HALF AN HOUR AHEAD...
• Start cooking the lentils.
• Prepare the salad appetizer and let stand.
• Cook the sausages and combine with the lentils; keep warm.

JUST BEFORE SERVING...
• Finish the salad and serve.
• Take the lemon possets out of the refrigerator and set aside at room temperature.
• Serve up the sausages and lentils.
• Serve the lemon possets.

VINE TOMATO & BREAD SALAD

Italians often make this salad as a way of using up stale or 'day-old' bread—they call it panzanella. The bread brilliantly soaks up the sweet and tangy juices from the tomatoes and the extra virgin olive oil. We used ciabatta rolls, but any good rustic bread will do.

4 servings

6–8 slices of leftover bread
6 large ripe vine tomatoes
1 red onion, peeled and thinly sliced
juice of ½ lime
6 tbsp extra virgin olive oil
sea salt and freshly ground black pepper
pinch of superfine sugar (optional)
handful of Italian parsley

TIP As the intention of the dish is to use up leftover bread, there is no need for precision—use whatever type or amount of bread you have on hand and adjust the tomatoes and dressing according to taste.

Tear the bread into bite-size pieces and place in a large bowl. Cut the tomatoes into wedges and add them to the bowl with the red onion. Drizzle with the lime juice and olive oil. Season with salt and pepper, then toss well. Let stand for 15 minutes to allow the flavors to mingle together.

Taste and adjust the seasoning, adding a little more lime juice if you prefer a sharper taste, or a pinch of sugar if the salad is too tart.

Tear the leaves from the parsley and toss them with the salad just before serving.

ITALIAN SAUSAGES WITH LENTILS

" In Italy, sausages are served with lentils as part of a traditional New Year's meal, rather than something you would resort to for a fry-up. I think they make the ideal family meal—quick, easy, and very tasty. Try to get good quality sausages, such as Genovese, from an Italian deli and use the right kind of lentils that will hold their shape after cooking—ideally little brown Castelluccio lentils from Umbria or French Puy lentils. "

4 servings

olive oil, for cooking
7oz (200g) smoked bacon, cut into small
   cubes
1 onion, peeled and minced
1 medium carrot, peeled and cut into
   ½-inch (1-cm) cubes
3 bay leaves
1lb (450g) Castelluccio or Puy lentils,
   rinsed and drained
sea salt and freshly ground black pepper
1 large garlic clove, peeled and smashed
12 Italian sausages
⅓ cup (100ml) dry white wine
handful of Italian parsley, leaves
   chopped

Heat a little olive oil in a heavy pan and sauté the bacon until lightly golden, about 5 minutes. Add the onion, carrot, and bay leaves, stir well, and cook over medium heat for 5 to 6 minutes until the onions begin to soften.

Tip in the lentils, stir well, and pour in enough water to cover. Bring to a boil, lower the heat, and simmer, covered, for 25 to 30 minutes until most of the liquid has been absorbed and the lentils are tender. Season generously with salt and pepper.

Cook the sausages in the meantime. Heat a little olive oil in a heavy skillet. Add the garlic and cook for a minute. Add the sausages and pan-fry for about 5 minutes, turning occasionally, until lightly golden. Deglaze the pan with the white wine and bring to a boil. Lower the heat to a simmer, and let the sausages braise for 15 to 20 minutes until cooked through.

With a pair of tongs, transfer the sausages to the lentils, nestling them among the vegetables and lentils and adding the pan juices. Reheat for a few more minutes.

Divide the lentils and sausages among warm shallow bowls. Sprinkle generously with chopped parsley and a grinding of black pepper, then serve.

LEMON POSSET

> " Lemon posset is delightfully simple, tangy, and very rich, so a little goes a long way. We serve it in shot glasses with long, thin cookies on the side for dipping. To make a lighter dessert, you could fold through some Italian meringue to aerate the dense lemon cream. "

4 servings

1¼ cups (300ml) heavy cream
⅜ cup (75g) superfine sugar
juice of 1–2 lemons
langues de chats or almond cookies,
   to serve

Pour the cream into a small pan and add the sugar. Slowly bring to a boil, stirring constantly to dissolve the sugar. Once it comes to a boil, let the cream bubble for another 3 minutes, stirring all the time.

Remove the pan from the heat and pour in the juice of 1 lemon, stirring the mixture thoroughly as you do so. It should start to thicken instantly. Taste the mixture and add a little more lemon juice if it's not tart enough. The posset should be sweet, tangy, and creamy.

Let cool for about 5 minutes, then pour into individual glasses. Cover with plastic wrap and chill in the refrigerator for at least 3 hours or overnight. If the possets are very firm, take them out of the refrigerator 15 minutes before serving to soften. Serve with dessert cookies.

5 ways with...GREENS

Braised kale with pancetta
Serves 4

Trim and chop 1lb (500g) kale. Sauté 5oz (150g) chopped pancetta with 2 tbsp olive oil in a large pan until golden brown. Stir in the chopped kale, add ⅓ cup (100ml) chicken or vegetable stock and season well. Cook over high heat for a few minutes, stirring frequently, until the kale is wilted and tender. Taste and adjust the seasoning, then serve. Delicious with poultry, fish, or meat dishes.

Sautéed spinach with nutmeg
Serves 4–6

Heat 2 tbsp olive oil in a large pan. Tip in 1⅓lb (600g) washed baby leaf spinach leaves and stir over high heat until just wilted. (You may need to cook the spinach in two batches if your pan is not wide enough.) Season with salt, pepper, and a little grated nutmeg and serve immediately. An excellent base for fish, vegetarian, or beef dishes.

Cavolo nero with garlic & chile
Serves 4–6

Remove the stems from 2 bunches of cavolo nero and finely shred the leaves. Heat 2 tbsp olive oil in a large pan and gently sauté 1 thinly sliced medium onion and 2 thinly sliced garlic cloves until the onions begin to soften. Stir in 1 minced, seeded red chile and cook for another minute. Add the cavolo nero and sauté for 4 to 5 minutes or until wilted. Season generously with salt and pepper and serve immediately. A great side dish to Italian-style fish, chicken, veal, or pork dishes.

176

Purple sprouting broccoli with pine nuts & sesame seeds
Serves 4–6

Trim 2lb (1kg) purple sprouting broccoli and cut into 2-inch (5-cm) lengths. Blanch in a pan of boiling salted water for a couple of minutes until *al dente*, then refresh under cold running water and drain well. Heat 3–4 tbsp olive oil in a large pan and add a couple of pieces of butter. Toss in the broccoli, warm through, and season with salt and pepper to taste. Finally toss in 2 tbsp toasted pine nuts and 1–2 tbsp toasted sesame seeds. Serve warm as an accompaniment to chicken, pork, or pasta.

Watercress & spinach purée
Serves 4–6

Trim 10oz (300g) watercress and 4oz (100g) spinach leaves. Blanch the watercress in a pan of boiling salted water for 5 minutes, then add the spinach leaves and wilt for a minute. Drain in a colander and press with the back of a ladle or spoon to extract as much liquid as possible. For a drier result, wrap in a clean cloth and squeeze out the liquid. Whiz the green pulp in a food processor to a smooth purée, scraping down the sides a few times. With the motor running, pour in 4 tbsp heavy cream and blend for several minutes until the purée is very smooth. Season to taste with salt and pepper. Use as a garnish for beef or fish dishes.

19 Retro dining

Revive well-loved classics for a nostalgic family meal that's guaranteed to appeal. Most of the preparation for each course can be done well in advance, leaving you plenty of time to relax with family and friends before the meal. This menu serves 4.

Horseradish marinated salmon

Beef wellington
+ Wilted Boston lettuce
+ Sautéed potatoes with thyme & garlic

Gordon's trifle

planning your menu

A DAY AHEAD...
• Prepare the marinated salmon and keep well wrapped in the refrigerator.
• Make the trifle (but not the topping), cover, and refrigerate.

SEVERAL HOURS IN ADVANCE...
• Drain the salmon, rinse off marinade, and coat in the horseradish cream. Wrap and chill. Make the balsamic dressing too.
• Prepare the beef tenderloin, wrapping it in the mushroom paste, prosciutto, and outer plastic wrap. Refrigerate.

TWO HOURS AHEAD...
• Wrap the beef in the pastry; chill again.
• Peel and parboil the potatoes. Drain and toss in olive oil.
• Prepare the lettuce ready for cooking.
• Make the crème fraîche topping and spread on top of the trifle. Make the peanut brittle and set aside.

AROUND 40 MINUTES AHEAD...
• Glaze the pastry and put the beef wellington in the oven to cook.
• Crush the peanut brittle, ready for the trifle.

ABOUT 15 MINUTES AHEAD...
• Slice the salmon and plate the appetizer.
• Sauté the potatoes; keep warm.

JUST BEFORE SERVING...
• Dress the salmon and serve.
• Rest the beef while you eat the appetizer.
• Wilt the lettuce, carve the beef, and serve the main course.
• Sprinkle the peanut brittle over the trifle and serve.

HORSERADISH MARINATED SALMON

" This is similar to curing salmon for gravadlax, though I add some horseradish, which gives it a slight peppery kick. Instead of the balsamic dressing, you could serve mayonnaise spiked with a little horseradish as a creamy sauce on the side. "

4 servings

1lb 2oz (500g) salmon fillet, skinned
2–3 tbsp coarse sea salt
freshly ground black pepper
2–3 tbsp granulated sugar
2–3 tbsp creamed horseradish
large handful of dill, parsley, and
   cilantro sprigs, chopped

DRESSING:
1 tbsp balsamic vinegar
1 tbsp Dijon mustard
3 tbsp olive oil
sea salt and freshly ground black pepper

Trim the salmon, removing any fins and cutting away any bands of pale fat at the edges. Run your fingers over the fish to check for small bones and use tweezers to remove any you come across.

Mix the salt, pepper, and sugar together and rub this mixture all over the salmon. Wrap in plastic wrap, lay in a shallow dish, and refrigerate overnight.

Pour away any liquid that exudes from the salmon. Unwrap the fillet and rinse off the marinade, then pat dry with paper towels. Brush the skinned side with a thin layer of horseradish cream and coat with the chopped herbs. Wrap tightly in plastic wrap and chill until ready to serve.

Holding the knife at a 45° angle, slice the marinated salmon as thinly as possible. Fan out the salmon slices on individual serving plates.

For the dressing, whisk the balsamic vinegar, mustard, and olive oil together and season with salt and pepper to taste. Drizzle over the salmon to serve.

BEEF WELLINGTON

" This is an impressive dish and one that's easier than it looks. To keep the pastry light and crisp, we wrap the beef and mushrooms in a layer of prosciutto—to shield the dough from moisture. You could take it further and add a layer of thin crêpes (see page 249). "

4 servings

14oz (400g) flat cap mushrooms, roughly
  chopped
sea salt and freshly ground black pepper
olive oil, for cooking
1½–¾lb (750g) piece of prime beef
  tenderloin
1–2 tbsp English mustard
6–8 slices of prosciutto
1lb 2oz (500g) ready-made puff pastry
flour, to dust
2 egg yolks, beaten

Put the mushrooms into a food processor with
some seasoning and pulse to a rough paste. Scrape the paste into a pan and cook over high heat for about 10 minutes, tossing frequently, to cook out the moisture from the mushrooms. Spread out on a plate to cool.

Heat a skillet and add a little olive oil. Season the beef and
sear in the hot pan for 30 seconds only on each side. (You don't want to cook it at this stage, just color it.) Remove the beef from the skillet and let cool, then brush all over with the mustard.

Lay a sheet of plastic wrap on a counter and arrange the
prosciutto slices on it, in slightly overlapping rows. With a spatula or palette knife, spread the mushroom paste over the ham, then place the seared beef tenderloin in the middle. Keeping a tight hold of the plastic wrap from the edge, neatly roll the prosciutto and mushrooms around the beef to form a tight barrel shape. Twist the ends of the plastic wrap to secure. Chill for 15 to 20 minutes to let the beef set and keep its shape.

Roll out the puff pastry on a floured surface
to a large rectangle, about ⅛ inch (3mm) thick. Remove the plastic wrap from the beef, then lay in the center. Brush the surrounding pastry with egg yolk. Fold the ends over, then wrap the pastry around the beef, cutting off any excess. Turn over, so the seam is underneath, and place on a baking sheet. Brush all over the pastry with egg and chill for about 15 minutes to let the pastry rest. Heat the oven to 400°F (200°C).

Lightly score the pastry at ½ inch (1cm)
intervals and glaze again with beaten egg yolk. Bake for 20 minutes, then lower the oven setting to 350°F (180°C) and cook for another 15 minutes. Let rest for 10 to 15 minutes before slicing and serving with the accompaniments. The beef should still be pink in the center when you serve it.

Wilted Boston lettuce

Take the larger leaves from the lettuce (saving the smaller innermost ones for salads). Heat a little olive oil in a pan. Add the lettuce leaves and quickly sauté with a sprinkling of salt and pepper over high heat just enough to wilt them—less than a minute. Serve at once.

4 servings
2 large Boston lettuce, trimmed
a little olive oil, for cooking
sea salt and freshly ground black pepper

Sautéed potatoes with thyme & garlic

4 servings
4 large potatoes, about 1lb 2oz (500g) in total, peeled
sea salt and freshly ground black pepper
olive oil, for cooking
1 head of garlic (unpeeled), halved horizontally
1 thyme sprig

Parboil the potatoes in salted water for 10 to 12 minutes. Drain well and quarter lengthwise. Heat a little olive oil in a skillet. Sauté the potatoes with the garlic and thyme until golden brown, crisp on the outside, and cooked through. Remove the thyme and garlic, season well, and serve.

183

GORDON'S TRIFLE

"With the right combination of textures and flavors, a trifle can be very tempting. We vary the fruit between the layers of liqueur-soaked sponge and vanilla custard according to the season. To top it off, a sprinkling of crushed, salted peanut brittle balances out the sweetness and adds crunch."

4–6 servings

CUSTARD:
1¾ cups (400ml) milk
½ cup (120ml) heavy cream
1 vanilla bean, split
6 egg yolks
⅓ cup (60g) superfine sugar
1 tbsp cornstarch

TRIFLE:
2 tbsp brown sugar
4 peaches, pitted and sliced into wedges
few pieces of unsalted butter
4–5 tbsp Grand Marnier, or to taste
1 large jelly-filled jelly roll, cut into ½-inch (1-cm) slices

TOPPING:
2x 7oz (200g) tubs of crème fraîche
1 tbsp brown sugar
1 vanilla bean, split
oil, to oil
2 tbsp superfine sugar
⅔ cup (100g) salted peanuts (or unsalted if you prefer)

To make the custard, put the milk and cream into a heavy pan with the seeds from the vanilla bean. Heat gently to infuse. In a large bowl, whisk together the egg yolks, sugar, and cornstarch. When the cream begins to bubble up the sides of the pan, take off the heat and slowly pour onto the eggs, whisking all the time. Pour through a fine strainer back into the hot pan. Return to medium-low heat and keep whisking until the custard thickens. Set aside to cool.

For the trifle, melt the brown sugar in a wide nonstick pan over medium heat, swirling it around as it begins to caramelize. Add the peaches, toss to mix, and allow to take on a little color before adding a few pieces of butter. Sprinkle with 2 tbsp Grand Marnier and let bubble until the liqueur has reduced right down and the fruit is tender, but retaining its shape. Let cool.

Line the bottom of a large serving bowl with the jelly roll slices and drizzle with 2–3 tbsp Grand Marnier. Spoon the caramelized fruit on top, followed by the custard. Cover the bowl with plastic wrap and chill for least 2 hours or overnight (the longer the better).

For the topping, mix the crème fraîche with the brown sugar. Add the seeds from the vanilla bean and stir until evenly combined. Spread on top of the trifle and refrigerate while you prepare the peanut brittle. Have ready a lightly oiled baking sheet. Toss the superfine sugar and peanuts in a dry nonstick pan over high heat to caramelize the sugar and toast the peanuts. When the caramel turns golden brown, tip the mixture onto the baking sheet in a single layer. Let cool and set, then crush roughly in a large bowl with the end of a rolling pin.

Just before serving, scatter the peanut brittle evenly over the top of the trifle.

185

20 Sole food

Savor the fabulous aromas that this easy-to-prepare light menu offers and you will return to it time and time again. Sautéed spinach with nutmeg (see page 176) is a good alternative to the red chard accompaniment. This menu serves 4.

Spring garden soup

Sole en papillote

+ Sautéed red chard with garlic
+ Minted new potatoes

Apple tarte fine with rum & raisin ice cream

planning your menu

A FEW DAYS AHEAD...
• Order the sole from the fish supplier and ask him to fillet it for you (arranging to collect it a day ahead, or fresh on the day if you can).

THE DAY BEFORE...
• Make the ice cream and freeze.

TWO HOURS AHEAD...
• Prepare the apple purée and refrigerate (or do this the day before).
• Prepare the veg for the soup, set aside.
• Scrub the potatoes and immerse in cold water.
• Prepare the chard so it's ready to cook.
• Shape and bake the pastry disks for the apple tarts.

AN HOUR AHEAD...
• Slice the apples and assemble the tarts; chill.
• Assemble the sole packages, ready to cook.
• Make the spring garden soup.
• Blanch and refresh the chard so it's ready to cook.
• Bake the tarts for 5 minutes, then cool for 5 minutes.

JUST BEFORE SERVING...
• Ladle the soup into bowls, top with mint, and serve.
• Put the sole packages into the oven and cook the potatoes while you eat the appetizer.
• Sauté the chard, dress the potatoes, and serve the main course.
• Put the apple tarts into the oven to finish baking while you eat the main course.
• Glaze the tarts and serve topped with a scoop of ice cream.

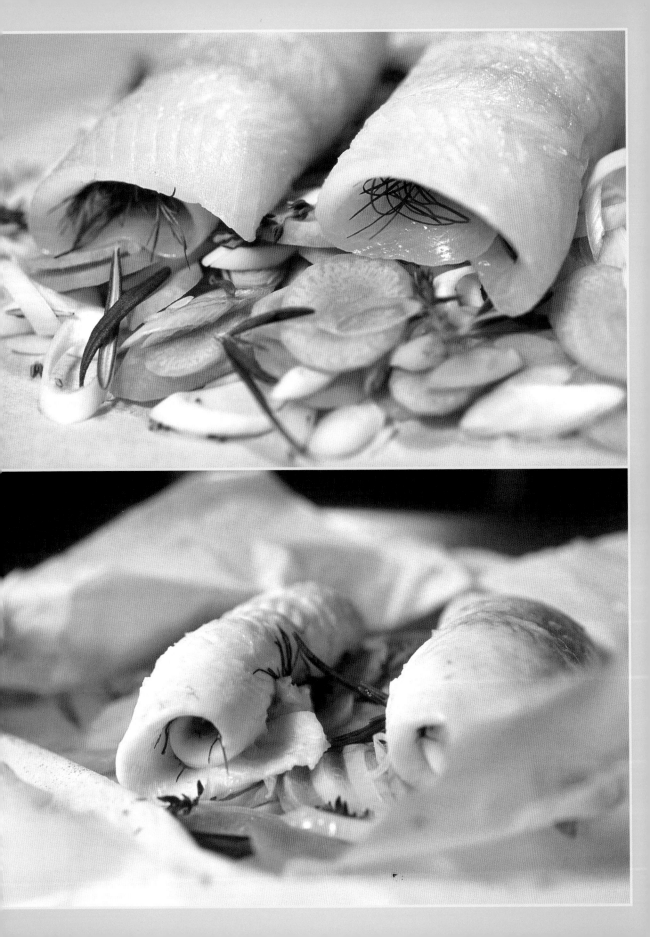

SPRING GARDEN SOUP

66 This colorful soup makes the most of spring vegetables. These are chopped and gently 'sweated' in a little olive oil before any liquid is added to the pan to encourage them to release their natural juices and gives the final broth a full flavor. If you like, you can add a spoonful of grated Parmesan at the end, to thicken the soup slightly and provide extra savoriness. 99

4 servings

5oz (150g) unsmoked bacon, cut into small cubes
olive oil, for cooking
1 onion, peeled and chopped
4oz (100g) baby leeks, trimmed and chopped
4oz (100g) baby carrots, scrubbed and roughly chopped
2 small turnips, about 6oz (175g), peeled and cut into ½-inch (1-cm) cubes
1 large potato, about 5oz (150g), peeled and cut into ½-inch (1-cm) cubes
4oz (100g) green beans, trimmed and cut into ¾–1¼-inch (2–3-cm) sticks
¼ savoy cabbage, cored and chopped
sea salt and freshly ground black pepper
handful of mint leaves, chopped

In a large pan, sauté the bacon in a little olive oil for 3 to 4 minutes until lightly golden. Add the onion and leeks and cook for a few more minutes. Stir in the chopped carrots, turnips, and potato. Cover the pan with a lid and sweat the vegetables for 4 to 5 minutes until soft and translucent. Meanwhile, put the kettle on to boil.

Pour boiling water into the pan to cover the vegetables (about 5 cups/1.2 liters). Add the green beans and cook for about 2 minutes. Finally throw in the chopped cabbage and simmer for 2 minutes or until it has wilted. Season to taste with salt and pepper.

Ladle the soup into warm bowls and sprinkle with freshly chopped mint to serve.

SOLE EN PAPILLOTTE

" Lemon sole has a soft texture and subtle flavor. It is ideally suited to cooking *en papillotte*, as the fish gentle steams in the parcel helping to preserve its delicate qualities. Do slice the vegetables thinly as they will need to cook at the same rate as the sole. "

4 servings

2 small carrots, peeled
2 small leeks, white part only
3–4 scallions, trimmed
4–5 garlic cloves (unpeeled), halved
few rosemary sprigs, leaves only
few thyme sprigs
8 skinned lemon sole fillets, about
   5–6oz (150–175g) each
sea salt and freshly ground black pepper
few dill sprigs
olive oil, to drizzle
about ⅓ cup (100ml) dry white wine

Heat the oven to 400°F (200°C). Cut out eight large squares of baking parchment, measuring about 12 by 12 inches (30 by 30cm). Thinly slice the carrots, leeks, and scallions on the diagonal. Tip the vegetables and garlic into a bowl, add the rosemary and thyme, and toss to mix. Scatter the mixture in neat piles in the center of four of the parchment sheets.

Season each sole fillet with salt and pepper and place a few dill sprigs on top. Roll up the fillets, enclosing the dill and place two rolled fillets on each pile of vegetables. Drizzle with olive oil and sprinkle with salt and pepper.

Place another sheet of paper on top of each package and using short folds, secure the edges to seal in the fish and vegetables. When you've reached the last fold, carefully pour in a generous splash of white wine and a little water. Seal the packages and place on one or two large baking sheets. Bake for 20 minutes or until the lemon sole feels firm in the middle.

Lift the packages onto warm large plates. Bring to the table and cut a cross in the center of the parchment with kitchen scissors open the parcels. Accompany with sautéed red chard and minted new potatoes if you wish.

sautéed red chard with garlic

Roughly chop the chard and separate the [stalks] from the leaves. Bring a pan of salted water to a boil. Blanch the [stalks] for 3 to 5 minutes, then add the leaves and cook for another minute. [Refresh] under cold running water and drain well. When ready to serve, [heat] a little olive oil in a pan and add the garlic. When it begins to turn [golden], toss in the chard. Season well and cook for 2 to 3 minutes until the [chard] is tender. Serve warm.

4 servings

1 large red chard, about 2¼lb (1kg)
sea salt and freshly ground black pepper
olive oil, for cooking
3 garlic cloves, peeled and minced

minted new potatoes

[se]rvings
[1]2oz (500g) new potatoes, washed
[sea] salt and freshly ground black pepper
[sma]ll bunch of mint
[3]tbsp Classic vinaigrette (see page 247)
[fine]ly grated zest of 1 lemon

Scrub the potatoes and cut any larger ones in half. Place in a large pan and add cold water to cover. Add a large pinch of salt and the stalks from the bunch of mint. Partially cover with a lid and simmer for 15 to 20 minutes until the potatoes are just tender when pierced with a skewer. Meanwhile, shred the mint leaves. Drain the potatoes and toss with the vinaigrette, salt, and pepper while still warm. Sprinkle with the shredded mint and lemon zest to serve.

APPLE TARTE FINE WITH RUM & RAISIN ICE CREA

" This classic tart is quite time-consuming to make, but well worth the effort. We contrast our warm apple tarts with homemade rum and raisin (actually golden raisin) ic cream. To save time, you could just fold some rum-soaked golden raisins through a tub good-quality ready-made vanilla ice cream. "

4–6 servings

RUM AND "RAISIN" ICE CREAM:
½ cup (85g) golden raisins
about ⅓ cup (100ml) white rum
1 quantity Crème anglaise (see page 248)

APPLE PURÉE:
2 medium cooking apples, about 1lb 2oz (500g) in total
4 tbsp golden superfine sugar, or more to taste
¼ tsp ground cinnamon
squeeze of lemon juice

TART:
1lb 2oz (500g) ready-made puff pastry
flour, to dust
3–4 Granny Smith or Braeburn apples
1½ tbsp (20g) unsalted butter, melted, plus extra to grease
1–2 tbsp golden superfine sugar, to sprinkle
2 tbsp apricot jelly, warmed with 1 tbsp water

For the ice cream, put the golden raisins and rum into a small pan, bring to a boil, then take off the heat and set aside to soa preferably overnight. Churn the crème anglaise in an ice cream machine u slushy. Add the golden raisins with the rum and continue churning until the cream is firm. Transfer to a plastic container and freeze.

For the apple purée, peel, core, and chop the apples. Place in a pan with the sugar, cinnamon, lemon juice, and 4 tbsp water. Stir and bring to a boil. Lower the heat, cover, and cook gently for 10 minutes or until the apples are soft. Taste and add a little more sugar if apples are too tart. Push through a fine strainer and let cool.

Heat the oven to 400°F (200°C). Roll out the puff past thinly on a lightly floured surface to a ¹⁄₁₆ inch (2mm) thickness. Using a 5-inch (13-cm) plate or saucer as a guide, cut out 4–6 circles and place on two large baking sheets lined with baking parchment. Peel, core, and thinly slice the apples.

Spread a thin layer of apple purée over the past disks, leaving a ½–¾-inch (1–2-cm) margin. Arrange the apple slices in a circle on top of the purée, overlapping them slightly. Brush them with melte butter and sprinkle with a fine layer of sugar. Chill for 15 to 20 minutes.

Bake the tarts for 5 minutes, then let cool for 5 minutes Cover each sheet of tarts with lightly greased baking parchment and weigh down with another baking sheet. Holding the sandwiched baking sheets tightly, flip them so the pastries are on top of the apples. Bake for another 15 to 20 minutes until the pastry is brown and crisp.

Flip the baking sheets carefully again as you remove them from the oven. Transfer the tarts to a wire rack and brush wit the warm apricot jelly to glaze. Serve them warm, with a scoop of ice crea

5 ways with...CARROTS

Carrot, beet & orange salad
Serves 4–6

Peel and grate 1lb (500g) carrots and ½lb (250g) cooked beet. Put into a bowl with 3 peeled and segmented oranges, a small handful of chives, and 4–5 tbsp Classic vinaigrette (see page 247). Quickly toss all the ingredients together, but avoid overmixing. Serve as a barbecue accompaniment or as part of a light appetizer.

Carrot purée
Serves 4

Peel and thickly slice 1½lb (750g) carrots and cook in boiling salted water for 5 to 7 minutes or until tender. Drain well, reserving the cooking liquid. Whiz the carrots fine purée in a food processor, adding 1–2 tbsp cooking liquor to get them moving and scraping down the sides a few times. For a smooth result, push the purée through a fine strainer. Reheat just before serving, adding a few pieces of butter a seasoning to taste. A tasty base on which to serve chicken breasts or monkfish.

Pan-roasted carrots with gremolata
Serves 4–6

Scrub 1½lb (750g) baby carrots. Melt 2 tbsp (30g) unsalted butter in a pan, add th carrots with a little salt and pepper, and cook over medium heat, tossing occasiona until just tender. Meanwhile, to make the gremolata, mince a handful of Italian pars leaves and mix with 2 tsp finely crushed garlic, 2 tsp finely grated lemon zest, 2 tb olive oil, and some seasoning. Scatter over the carrots as you serve them. Deliciou warm or at room temperature, with lightly spiced fish, chicken, or pasta.

Glazed carrots with rosemary

rves 4–6

Peel 1½–2lb (750g–1kg) medium carrots and parboil them in salted water for 7 to 9 minutes. Drain and refresh under cold running water. When ready to serve, melt 2 tbsp (30g) unsalted butter in a wide sauté pan, add the carrots with a few sprigs of rosemary, and toss over high heat until the carrots are golden and coated in a buttery glaze. Sprinkle with salt and pepper and serve warm. A great accompaniment to roast meats.

piced carrots with star anise

rves 4–6

Peel 2¼lb (1kg) medium carrots (about 12), quarter lengthwise, then cut into 2¾–3¼-inch (7–8-cm) sticks. Melt 2 tbsp (30g) unsalted butter in a heavy pan over medium heat. When it begins to foam, add the carrot sticks and sauté for 5 minutes until slightly softened. Sprinkle with 2 tbsp soft brown sugar, a squeeze of lemon juice, 4–5 star anise, ¼ tsp ground cinnamon, and a pinch of cayenne pepper if you like. Add ½ cup (120ml) water (or vegetable stock) and simmer until the carrots are tender and the liquid is reduced to a syrupy glaze. This may take up to 10 minutes. Season with salt and pepper to taste. Serve with Moroccan-style tagines, casseroles, or hearty fish dishes.

Wild garlic & parsley risotto
Chicken with petits pois à la française
Strawberry, peach & ginger crumble

SEVERAL HOURS IN ADVANCE...

• For the dessert, cook the fruit and let cool. Prepare the crumble topping.

AN HOUR AHEAD...

• Cook the chicken and reduce the stock; set aside ready to assemble.

• Prepare the ingredients for the petit pois and sauté the onions; set aside.

30 MINUTES AHEAD...

• Assemble the crumbles, ready to bake.

• Make the risotto.

• Put the crumbles into the oven.

• Add the stock and peas to the pearl onions and let simmer gently while you have the appetizer.

JUST BEFORE SERVING...

• Plate the risotto and serve.

• Return the chicken pieces to the sauce and reheat gently while you finish the petit pois.

• Take the desserts out of the oven and let stand.

• Plate the main course and serve.

• Serve the dessert.

WILD GARLIC & PARSLEY RISOTTO

66 Wild garlic is at its best during spring when it is mild-tasting but incredibly fragrant. When you make this risotto, rather than discard the parsley stalks, add them to the hot stock to impart flavor. The chopped parsley leaves should be added right at the end, to keep their vibrant color. 99

4 servings

5½ cups (1.3 liters) Chicken (or vegetable) stock (see page 246)
3 tbsp olive oil, plus extra to drizzle
3–4 wild garlic cloves (or new season's garlic), sliced
4 shallots, peeled and minced
scant 1⅔ cups (350g) risotto rice, such as Carnaroli
sea salt and freshly ground black pepper
few pieces of butter
4oz (100g) Parmesan, freshly grated, plus shavings to serve
handful of Italian parsley, leaves chopped

Bring the stock to a simmer in a pan and keep it at a simmer over low heat.

Heat the olive oil in a larger pan and add the garlic, followed by the shallots. Cook for 2 to 3 minutes until the shallots have softened. Stir in the rice and cook for a couple of minutes until the rice grains appear translucent, stirring frequently.

A ladleful at a time, add the hot stock to the rice and cook, stirring, until almost all the liquid is absorbed before adding the next ladleful. When you have added most of the stock (you may not need all of it), season and taste the rice. It should be *al dente*, cooked but with a bite in the center. Take the pan off the heat.

Stir the butter into the risotto, followed by the grated Parmesan and chopped parsley. Add a splash more stock to keep the rice moist and creamy if you like. Serve at once, scattered with Parmesan shavings and topped with a drizzle of olive oil.

CHICKEN WITH PETITS POIS A LA FRANÇAISE

> *My version of a chicken fricassée pairs the tender chicken with sweet, braised peas, rather than a creamy mushroom sauce, for an altogether lighter affair.*

4 servings

1 chicken, about 3lb 5oz –4½lb (1.5–2kg)
3 tbsp all-purpose flour
sea salt and freshly ground black pepper
2–3 tbsp olive oil
2 carrots, cut into ½-inch (1-cm) cubes
2 celery stalks, cut into ½-inch (1-cm) cubes
1 large onion, peeled and minced
2 garlic cloves, peeled and chopped
few thyme sprigs
2 bay leaves
⅔ cup (150ml) dry white wine
3⅓–3½ cups (800–900ml) Chicken stock (see page 246)
handful of Italian parsley, chopped

PETIT POIS A LA FRANÇAISE:
2 tbsp olive oil
5oz (150g) small pearl onions, peeled
few thyme sprigs
1 bay leaf
⅓ cup (100ml) Chicken stock (page 246)
1lb 2oz (500g) young fresh peas
4 tbsp (50g) butter, cut into cubes
2 Boston lettuce, shredded

TIP Chicken breasts take less time to cook than the other pieces. To keep them succulent, take them out after 20 minutes' cooking and warm through in the sauce at the end.

Joint the chicken into eight pieces. Season the flour with salt and pepper and toss the chicken pieces in it to coat all over. Heat a little olive oil in a wide skillet and cook the chicken pieces, in two batches, over medium heat until golden brown on all sides. Remove the chicken with a slotted spoon and set aside on a plate.

Add the carrots, celery, onion, garlic, thyme, and bay leaves to the pan. Stir and cook over medium heat for 4 to 5 minutes until the vegetables are beginning to soften. Pour in the white wine, scraping the bottom of the pan with a wooden spoon to deglaze. Return the chicken pieces to the pan, nestling them among the vegetables, and pour in enough stock to cover. Bring to a boil, then reduce the heat to a low simmer. Skim off any scum that rises to the surface, put the lid on the pan and simmer gently for 30 to 40 minutes until the chicken is tender.

With a pair of tongs, remove the chicken from the pan and set aside. Strain the stock through a fine strainer, pushing with the back of a wooden spoon to extract as much juice from the vegetables as possible; discard the vegetables. Return the stock to a clean, wide pan. Skim off any excess fat from the top of the liquid, then let bubble for 10 to 15 minutes until reduced and thickened.

Cook the petit pois in the meantime. Heat the olive oil in a large, shallow pan. Add the pearl onions, thyme, and bay leaf and sauté over medium heat for 5 minutes. Add the stock, peas, and some salt and pepper. Simmer gently for 10 minutes until the vegetables are tender. Stir in the butter, a few pieces at a time, to enrich and help thicken the sauce. Finally, mix through the lettuce and heat briefly until wilted.

Return the chicken to the pan and reheat gently in the sauce for a few minutes. Serve with the peas and a generous sprinkling of chopped parsley.

STRAWBERRY, PEACH & GINGER CRUMBLE

" This is another lovely crumble, marrying together the delightful flavors of strawberry, peach, and ginger. The great thing about crumbles is that you can make them all year round—using different fruits as they come into season. "

4 servings

3 ripe peaches
generous 2 cups (300g) strawberries, hulled and quartered
2 pieces of preserved ginger in syrup, drained and minced
2 tbsp sugar

CRUMBLE:
⅓ cup (50g) toasted hazelnuts
½ cup (70g) all-purpose flour
pinch of ground cinnamon
2 tbsp (25g) cold butter, cut into pieces
¼ cup (50g) raw brown sugar
2 tbsp superfine sugar

TO SERVE:
pouring cream or Crème anglaise (see page 248)

Heat the oven to 400°F (200°C). Halve, pit, and roughly dice the peaches, then put them into a dry nonstick pan with the strawberries, ginger, sugar, and 2 tbsp water. Cook over high heat for 2 minutes until the fruit is slightly softened but not mushy. Tip into a bowl and let cool.

For the crumble, lightly crush the hazelnuts in a bowl with the end of a rolling pin. In a large mixing bowl, stir together the flour and cinnamon. Using the tips of your fingers, rub the butter into the flour until the mixture resembles coarse bread crumbs. Stir through the crushed hazelnuts and raw brown sugar.

Spoon the softened fruit into four wide ramekins or individual baking dishes. Top with the crumble mixture, scattering it evenly, and stand the dishes on a baking sheet. Bake for 15 to 20 minutes until the topping is golden brown and crisp.

Let the crumble stand for a few minutes before serving, with cream or crème anglaise.

"The important thing is to try and enjoy cooking. It shouldn't be something that you dread. What is there to be scared of? You only learn through making mistakes so they are not something to be afraid of. I still get it wrong sometimes and I am still learning new things — that doesn't stop and you shouldn't either. Keep going until the fear is gone!"

22 Christmas dinner

I love the magic of Christmas. We usually have a large gathering and I get everyone t join in with the cooking. The traditional turkey is always popular, but I prefer the othe courses to be less predictable. If you are unsure about oysters, start with Horseradis marinated salmon (see page 181), a great prepare-ahead recipe. This menu serves 6-

Champagne oysters with cucumber pappardelle
Herb buttered turkey with citrus bread crumbs

+ Golden roasted potatoes   + Honey glazed carrots

+ Glazed parsnips   + Sautéed Brussels sprouts with almonds

+ Devils on horseback   + Cranberry sauce   + Pan gravy

Hugh's chestnut & chocolate truffle cake

planning your menu

WELL IN ADVANCE...
- Order your turkey.
- Order oysters from your fish supplier.
- Make the cranberry sauce.

THE DAY BEFORE...
- Prepare the devils on horseback, ready for cooking; keep refrigerated.
- Make the herb butter and prepare the bread crumbs, ready for sautéeing. In the evening, stuff the turkey; keep chilled.

4 OR 5 HOURS IN ADVANCE...
- Bring the turkey to room temperature.

3 HOURS AHEAD...
- Put the turkey in the oven, remembering to baste it occasionally.
- Shuck the oysters for the appetizer.
- Prepare all the vegetables. Blanch the sprouts, carrots, and parsnips and keep immersed separately in chilled water. Toss the peeled potatoes in oil, ready to roast.

- Make the chestnut and truffle cake (or do this a day ahead if serving cold).
- Make the stock for the gravy.

AN HOUR AHEAD...
- Prepare the ingredients for the appetizer ready for cooking; keep the cucumber ribbons immersed in chilled water.
- Make the stock for the gravy.

ABOUT 15 MINUTES AHEAD...
- Sauté the bread crumbs and cook the devils on horseback; keep both warm.
- Put the potatoes in the oven.
- Assemble the appetizer.

JUST BEFORE SERVING...
- Rest the turkey while eating the appetizer.
- Finish cooking the carrots, parsnips, and sprouts. Finish the gravy.
- Carve the turkey and serve.
- Unmold the truffle cake and serve.

TIP   To shuck oysters, first check that all the oysters are alive by tapping them gently on the counter. They should close tightly—discard any that don't. Hold the oyster using a thick, folded dish towel with one hand and an oyster knife (or a blunt butter knife) in the other. Keeping the oyster level, stick the knife through the hinge of the oyster shell and wriggle it from side to side to cut through the hinge muscle. Push in the knife a little further then twist up to lift the top shell. Tip the oyster juice into a bowl and remove any pieces of shell from the oyster. Slide the knife along the bottom shell to cut through the muscle and release the oyster.

CHAMPAGNE OYSTERS
WITH CUCUMBER PAPPARDELLE

This refreshing soup makes a great appetizer before a substantial meal. Do have all the ingredients prepared before you start cooking as the cucumbers and oysters take no time to cook through. Shuck the oysters just before cooking to keep them as fresh as possible and save the juices as they'll be used to season the stock.

servings

- cups (2 liters) good vegetable stock
- ng cucumbers, peeled
- resh oysters
- e of ½ lemon
- up (100ml) heavy cream or crème
- iche
- oston lettuce, trimmed and finely
- redded
- dful of chives, chopped
- s of Champagne
- salt and freshly ground black pepper

Bring the stock to a boil in a large pan. Using a vegetable peeler, peel about 8–10 wide, thin ribbons (resembling pappardelle pasta) from each cucumber, avoiding the seeds in the middle.

Shuck the oysters and add the juices to the hot stock with a little lemon juice and the cream. Let the liquid come back to a boil, then add the cucumber ribbons and oysters. Cook for 30 seconds only, then take off the heat and stir in the lettuce and chives. Add the Champagne and check the seasoning.

Pile the cucumber strips into the middle of four warm bowls. Divide the oysters among the bowls and pour in the soup. Serve at once.

HERB BUTTERED TURKEY WITH CITRUS BREAD CRUMBS

66 It was a treat to raise our own turkeys for Christmas last year, even if it did test Tana's patience at times! It has given us a new meaning to good, organic food. 99

6–8 servings

1 large oven-ready turkey, about 11–12lb (5–5.5kg)
sea salt and freshly ground black pepper
2 large onions, peeled and halved
1 orange, halved
1 head of garlic (unpeeled), halved horizontally
few bay leaves
few thyme sprigs
olive oil, to drizzle

HERB BUTTER:
small bunch of Italian parsley, chopped
small bunch of tarragon, chopped
1 tbsp thyme leaves
1 cup (250g) butter, softened to room temperature
1 black truffle (optional)

CITRUS BREADCRUMBS:
½ loaf of day-old bread, about 10oz (300g), crusts removed
grated zest of 1 orange
grated zest of 1 lemon
olive oil, for cooking
2oz (50g) pancetta (about 7–8 slices), chopped
½ onion, peeled and finely diced
few thyme sprigs
1⅓ cups (200g) pine nuts
⅔ cup (150g) butter, cut into cubes
squeeze of lemon juice

For the herb butter, mix the chopped herbs i the softened butter. If using the truffle, finely slice and chop, then mix into herb butter. Season well and spoon the flavored butter into a pastry bag.

Holding the turkey with one hand and starting from the neck flap, use the fingers of your other hand to loosen the skin over the breasts without tearing the skin. Move your hand toward the low side of the breast and toward the thighs and separate the skin from the meat. You want to create a large pocket with which to stuff the herb butte Pipe the butter into the pockets over the breasts and thighs. Gently massage over the skin to spread the herb butter evenly.

Heat the oven to 425°F (220°C). Open up the cavity the turkey, season with salt and pepper, and stuff with the onions, orange garlic, bay leaves, and thyme sprigs. Tuck the legs under the neck skin t secure them in place, or tie with kitchen string. Place the turkey, breast s up, in a large roasting tray. Drizzle with a little olive oil and season well. Roast for 10 to 15 minutes until the skin is crisp and golden. Lower the o setting to 350°F (180°C) and cook for approximately 30 minutes per lb (k basting occasionally. To test that your turkey is cooked, skewer the thick part of the thigh and check that the juices are running clear, not at all pin

Meanwhile, make the bread crumbs. Tear the bread roughly and whiz to coarse crumbs in a food processor. Add the orange a lemon zests and season well. Pulse a few times until well mixed. Heat a little olive oil in a large skillet and sauté the pancetta for a minute. Toss i the onion, thyme, and pine nuts. Cook for 3 to 4 minutes before adding t butter around the edge of the pan. Let the butter foam and turn a golden brown before adding the bread crumbs. Mix and cook, tossing frequently, 5 minutes until the crumbs are toasted and golden. Squeeze over a little lemon juice, discard the thyme, and adjust the seasoning. Keep warm.

When ready, cover the turkey with foil and let rest for a least 20 minutes. Carve the breast and thighs and serve with the citrus bread crumbs, gravy, and other accompaniments.

an gravy

servings

sp vegetable oil

ey giblets

allots, peeled and chopped

y leaves

thyme sprigs

ack peppercorns

sp all-purpose flour

up (100ml) white wine

Heat the oil in a pan and cook the giblets until browned all over. Pour in 2½ cups (600ml) water, stirring to deglaze the pan and add the shallots, bay leaves, thyme, and peppercorns. Bring to a boil and skim off any scum from the surface. Lower the heat and simmer for 1 hour. Strain the stock through a strainer.

Pour off excess fat from the turkey roasting tray and set it over medium heat. Stir in the flour and cook for 2 minutes. Gradually whisk in the wine, then the strained stock and simmer for 15 minutes or until thickened to the consistency of light cream. Season to taste.

olden roasted potatoes

eat the oven to 425°F (220°C). Heat the duck fat or oil in urdy baking tray over medium heat. Add the potatoes with plenty of soning and turn until golden and crisp. Put the tray into the oven and roast 40 to 45 minutes until the potatoes are cooked through (they should give ly when pierced with a knife). Drain on paper towels and serve.

6–8 servings

3–4 tbsp duck fat or vegetable oil

3lb 5oz– 4lb (1.5–1.8kg) potatoes, such as
    round red or Charlotte, peeled

sea salt and freshly ground black pepper

autéed brussels sprouts with almonds

servings

1¾lb (750g) Brussels sprouts,
mmed

salt and freshly ground black pepper

pieces of butter

e oil, for cooking

up (75g) slivered almonds, toasted

Cook the Brussels sprouts in boiling salted water for 7 to 9 minutes, until slightly softened. Drain the sprouts, refresh under cold running water, and drain thoroughly.

Just before serving, heat a little butter and olive oil in a large sauté pan. Add the sprouts and sauté until tender, scattering over the slivered almonds toward the end of cooking to let them brown gently.

211

oney glazed carrots

Cook the carrots in boiling salted water until tender, about 7 to 9 minutes. Drain, refresh under cold running er, and drain well. Heat the butter in a large sauté pan. Add the ots, season with salt and pepper, drizzle over the honey, and toss to coat. Sauté until the carrots are well glazed. Serve at once.

6–8 servings

12–16 medium carrots, peeled
sea salt and freshly ground black pepper
4 tbsp (50g) salted butter
2 tbsp runny honey

lazed parsnips

servings

large parsnips, peeled and halved
ngthwise
salt and freshly ground black pepper
sp (50g) salted butter

Cook the parsnips in boiling salted water until just tender, about 7 to 9 minutes. Drain, refresh under cold running water, and drain well. Heat the butter in a large sauté pan. Add the parsnips, season, and toss well to coat. Sauté until they are caramelized at the edges. Sprinkle with pepper and serve at once.

evils on horseback

lice the bacon in half lengthwise, wrap each half around a ne, and secure with a toothpick. Pan-fry in the olive oil for 3 to 4 minutes, turning asionally, until the bacon is crisp and prunes have softened. Remove the thpicks and serve warm.

8 servings

8 slices of lean bacon
16 pitted prunes
2 tbsp olive oil

ranberry sauce

ervings

ted zest and juice of 1 orange
erous 2 cups (200g) fresh (or ozen) cranberries
up (100g) superfine sugar
nnamon stick

Put all the ingredients in a small pan and set over high heat. Cook for 5 to 7 minutes until the cranberries start to soften or burst. Transfer to a bowl and let cool. If making in advance, pour straight into a sterilized jar, seal while it is still warm, and refrigerate when cooled, for up to a week.

HUGH'S CHESTNUT & CHOCOLATE TRUFFLE CAKE

" This cake caused a stir in the kitchen when Sharon Osbourne declared it a winner against my chocolate hazelnut tart! I thought it only fair to readers to include Hugh's recipe in the book and he has kindly given me his blessing to do so. "

6–8 servings

9oz (250g) semisweet chocolate, broken into pieces
1⅛ cups (250g) unsalted butter, plus extra to grease
9oz (250g) peeled, cooked chestnuts
½ cup (125ml) whole milk
½ cup (125ml) light cream
4 large eggs, separated
⅔ cup (125g) superfine sugar

TO SERVE:
mascarpone or crème fraîche, to serve
handful of marrons glacé, chopped (optional)

TIP This heavenly cake is also delicious served with whipping cream flavored with brandy-soaked raisins.

Heat the oven to 325°F (170°C). Grease and line a 10-inch (25-cm) springform cake pan.

Melt the semisweet chocolate and butter together in a bain-marie (or a bowl set over a pan of barely simmering water) or directly in a heavy pan over very gentle heat. Take off the heat and cool slightly. In another pan, heat the chestnuts with the milk and cream until just boiling, then whiz to a rough purée in a food processor (or mash thoroughly with a potato masher).

Beat the eggs yolks and superfine sugar together until pale and smooth. Stir in the chocolate and the chestnut purée until you have a smooth, blended mixture.

Whisk the egg whites in a clean bowl until stiff. Carefully fold them into the chestnut mixture, then spoon into the prepared pan. Bake for 25 to 35 minutes until the cake has just set but still has a slight wobble in the middle. Let cool a little in the pan to allow it to firm up slightly.

Carefully release the pan and cut the warm cake into slices—it will be soft and mousse-like. Alternatively, leave it to go cold and it will firm up when set.

Slice the truffle cake and serve each portion with a dollop of mascarpone or crème fraîche and a scattering of chopped marrons glacé if you like.

23 Pig roast

This is a celebration of the pig in its different guises—a tasty terrine of ham, followed by two roasts, and a refreshing dessert to finish the meal. Serve either pork roast or go the whole hog and cook both! After all, leftovers make great sandwiches. Serves 6–8.

Ham hock persillade with piccalilli

Roast loin of pork with crisp crackling

Pressed pork flank

+ Caramelized apple wedges

+ Broccoli with red onions, capers & almonds

White chocolate panna cotta with Champagne granita

planning your menu

A FEW DAYS AHEAD...
• Order the meat from your butcher (arranging to collect it a day ahead).
• Make the piccalilli (this can be done well ahead and improves with keeping).

THE DAY BEFORE...
• Make the persillade and refrigerate.
• Prepare the granita and freeze.
• Make the panna cotta and chill.
• Slow-roast the pork flank, press, and refrigerate overnight. Make the gravy, cool, and chill.

TWO HOURS AHEAD...
• Prepare the pork loin so it is ready for roasting. Set aside at room temperature.

AN HOUR AHEAD...
• Take the pork flank out of the refrigerator to bring to room temperature.
• Roast the pork loin.
• Prepare the ingredients for the accompaniments, ready to cook.

JUST BEFORE SERVING...
• Unmold the persillade and slice, ready to serve with the piccalilli.
• Cut the pork flank into portions and put into a very hot oven to fast-roast.
• Rest the pork loin while you eat the appetizer.
• Rest the pork flank while you cook the accompaniments and reheat the gravy.
• Serve the main course.
• Unmold the panna cottas and serve with the granita and raspberries.

HAM HOCK PERSILLADE
WITH PICCALILLI

❝ When I opened my first restaurant, I couldn't afford to put expensive ingredients prime meats on the menu. Less popular cuts provided more flavor and better value for money. This cold terrine shows how a humble cut can be elevated to another division with careful cooking. It can also be served with crusty bread and salads as a lunch. ❞

6–8 servings

2 large ham hocks, about 2lb 10oz (1.2kg) each (see tip)
1 tsp coriander seeds
1 tsp black peppercorns
2 bay leaves
few thyme sprigs
2 tbsp small capers, rinsed and drained
2oz (50g) gherkins, rinsed and minced
handful of Italian parsley, minced
sea salt and freshly ground black pepper
2 gelatin leaves

TO SERVE:
Piccalilli (opposite)

TIP I use unsmoked or "green" ham hocks for this terrine, but you can use smoked hocks if you prefer. Smoked ham hocks will need to be soaked overnight in cold water to remove excess salt.

Put the ham hocks into a large pan and cover with cold water. Bring to a boil and boil steadily for 10 minutes, skimming off the scum that floats to the surface. Remove the hocks and discard the water.

Return the hocks to the rinsed-out pan along with the coriander seeds, peppercorns, bay leaves, and thyme. Cover with cold water and bring to a simmer. Let simmer gently for 2½ to 3 hours until the hocks are tender and the flesh flakes easily.

To keep them succulent, leave the hocks to cool in the liquid, then lift them out. Strain the liquor into a clean pan and boil for 10 to 15 minutes until reduced by half.

Line a terrine, 1.5-quart (1.5-liter) capacity, with a double layer of plastic wrap, leaving some excess draping over the sides. Peel off the skin, then flake the ham or cut into small chunks. Put into a large bowl with the capers, gherkins, and parsley. Mix well, seasoning with salt and pepper. Pile the mixture into the terrine and pat down evenly.

Soak the gelatin leaves in cold water for a few minutes to soften. Measure 1 cup (250ml) of the reduced stock and season lightly (saving the rest for soup). Squeeze out excess water, then add the gelatin leaves to the hot stock. Stir until dissolved, then pour into the terrine mold to just cover the filling. Gently tap the terrine to ease the stock into any gaps and top off with a little more stock if necessary. Cover with plastic wrap and weigh down with a similar-sized loaf pan (or a carton of milk). Chill overnight or until set.

To unmold the persillade, tug at the plastic wrap. Unwrap the persillade and cut into thick slices. Serve with the piccalilli.

218

iccalilli

Dissolve the salt in 4 cups (1 liter) cold water to make a
ne, then add the onions, shallots, and cauliflower. Top off with a little more water if
brine doesn't cover the vegetables. Give the vegetables a stir and put a plate on
to keep them submerged in the brine. Leave in a cool place overnight.

The next day, drain the vegetables and soak in several changes
cold water to remove excess salt; drain well. Dissolve the sugar in the cider
egar over low heat, then boil for 15 to 20 minutes until reduced by half. Top off
1 cup (250ml) water and return to a boil. In a bowl, combine the cornstarch,
stard, ginger, and turmeric. Add 2–3 tbsp of the reduced vinegar and stir to a
ooth paste. Whisk this into the rest of the vinegar and simmer for 5 minutes until
mixture thickens enough to lightly coat the back of a wooden spoon.

Add the vegetables to the vinegar, bring to a boil, and
mer for 3 minutes until *al dente*, tender but with a bite. Pack in clean, sterilized
er jars and seal while still warm. Store in a cool, dark cupboard for up to 1 month
refrigerate after opening. The flavor of the piccalilli improves with keeping.

Makes about 1.5 litres
¼ cup (50g) fine sea salt
10oz (300g) pearl or small pickling
   onions, peeled
10oz (300g) shallots, peeled
   and halved
1 small cauliflower, about 1lb
   (450g), trimmed and cut into
   small florets
¾ cup (150g) superfine sugar
2 cups (500ml) cider vinegar
2 tbsp cornstarch
2 tbsp dry English mustard
1½ tbsp ground ginger
1½ tbsp ground turmeric

219

ROAST LOIN OF PORK
WITH CRISP CRACKLING

" The secret to perfect crackling is oil, salt, and heat. The pork skin is scored, rubbed with olive oil, and a generous amount of sea salt, then subject to an initial blast of high heat. The heat is essential to getting the crackling off to a good start. All the pork needs then is a good, slow roast to keep the flesh juicy and succulent. **"**

6–8 servings

1 pork loin, about 3lb (1.3kg)
2 garlic cloves, peeled and minced
grated zest of 1 lemon
small handful of Italian parsley,
  leaves only
small handful of sage leaves
sea salt and freshly ground black pepper
olive oil, to drizzle

TIP A very sharp, clean Stanley knife (or craft knife) is the most effective tool to use for scoring the tough pork skin.

Heat the oven
to its maximum setting, probably 475°F (240°C). Score the pork skin in a criss-cross pattern at $\frac{3}{4}$ inch (2cm) intervals. Turn it, so the flesh side is facing upward, and cut a slit along the side of the loin to open it out like a butterfly. Sprinkle the garlic and lemon zest all over the flesh and scatter the parsley and sage leaves along the center. Sprinkle with salt and pepper.

Roll up the loin
and secure with kitchen string at $1\frac{1}{4}$–$1\frac{1}{2}$ inch (3–4cm) intervals. Place, skin side up, in a lightly oiled roasting pan. Pat the scored skin dry with paper towels, then rub with a generous drizzle of olive oil and a few large pinches of sea salt. Roast for 15 to 20 minutes until the skin is golden and starting to crisp. Turn the oven down to 350°F (180°C) and continue to roast, allowing 25 minutes per 1lb (450g), until the pork is cooked through and tender. Rest for 10 to 15 minutes before carving.

PRESSED PORK FLANK

66 Pork flank really needs long, slow-cooking to tenderize the meat. This recipe roasts the pork twice—first in a slow oven until the meat is fork tender, then in a very hot oven to produce a crispy and golden crackling. **99**

6–8 servings

3lb (1.3kg) pork flank, ideally in one piece
(see tip)
sea salt and freshly ground black pepper
olive oil, to drizzle
2 heads of garlic (unpeeled), halved
horizontally
handful of thyme sprigs
splash of white wine
scant 2 cups (450ml) Chicken stock
(see page 246)

TIP If you buy pork flank from a supermarket, it will most likely be rolled. If so, remove the string and unroll. Lay flat on a board, skin side down, and cut a slit through the thick end of the pork to open it out like a butterfly so that the meat is evenly thick throughout.

Heat the oven to 325°F (170°C). Season the pork fl with salt and pepper, then turn the pork flank over and score the skin wi a sharp knife. Rub all over with olive oil, salt, and pepper.

Place the garlic, halved side up, on a lightly oiled roasting tray and scatter over the thyme sprigs. Lay the pork flank on to fat side up. Trickle with a little more olive oil and sprinkle with a little mo sea salt. Add a splash of white wine, cover the tray with foil, and bake f 1½ hours. Remove the foil, baste the pork with the juices, and return to oven, uncovered, for another ½ to 1 hour until tender. Continue to baste the pork occasionally with the pan juices.

Transfer the pork to a clean roasting tray to co Place another tray on top and weigh down with a can to flatten the pork Let cool and leave for several hours or overnight in the refrigerator to set the shape.

To make a gravy, skim off the excess fat from the roasting tray, then place on the stove over medium heat. Deglaze with t chicken stock, scraping the bottom of the tray to release any sediment. steadily until reduced and thickened.

Heat the oven to the highest setting, probably 475° (240°C). Cut the pressed pork into individual portions or squares and pa the skin dry with paper towels. Place the pork squares, fat side up, in a roasting tray and drizzle with olive oil and a generous pinch of sea salt. Roast for 15 minutes until the skin is golden brown and crisp. Trim the sides of the pork pieces to neaten after roasting if you like.

Rest the pork for 5 minutes, then serve with the light gravy and accompaniments.

aramelized apple wedges

elt the butter in a wide nonstick skillet. Dredge
pples in the superfine sugar and add to the pan when the butter
s to foam. Sauté for 3 to 4 minutes on each side over medium
until golden brown and caramelized. Toss in the scallions and
on and serve warm.

6–8 servings

1½ tbsp (20g) unsalted butter

3–4 Braeburn apples, cored, peeled, and cut
  into wedges

¼ cup (50g) superfine sugar

1 scallion, trimmed and finely sliced

few tarragon sprigs, leaves chopped

occoli with red onions, capers & almonds

ervings

e heads of broccoli

olive oil, plus extra to drizzle

e red onion, peeled and roughly chopped

alt and freshly ground black pepper

bsp red wine vinegar

capers, rinsed and drained

toasted slivered almonds (optional)

Cut the broccoli into florets. Trim away the
fibrous skin from the stalks, then cut the tender core into small cubes.
Heat the olive oil in a skillet and cook the red onion over medium
heat, stirring occasionally, for 8 to 10 minutes until soft. Season with
salt and pepper, deglaze the pan with the wine vinegar, and cook for
a few more minutes. Meanwhile, blanch the broccoli in boiling salted
water for 2 minutes and drain well. Add to the onions along with the
capers and a little more olive oil. Adjust the seasoning to taste. Serve
warm with a scattering of slivered almonds if you like.

WHITE CHOCOLATE
PANNA COTTA WITH CHAMPAGNE GRANITA

" This may seem an unlikely combination, but the clean, crisp freshness of the granita really cuts through the richness of the white chocolate panna cotta. A great dessert for any season ... "

6–8 servings

CHAMPAGNE GRANITA:
⅝ cup (125g) superfine sugar
3 tbsp liquid glucose
squeeze of lemon juice
1 cup (250ml) Champagne

PANNA COTTA:
2½ cups (600ml) heavy cream
⅔ cup (150ml) milk
scant ⅓ cup (60g) superfine sugar
3 gelatin sheets
7oz (200g) white chocolate, broken into
   small pieces

TO SERVE:
generous ¾ cup (125g) raspberries
finely pared lemon zest (optional)

First, make the granita.
Put the sugar, 1 cup (250ml) water, the liquid glucose, and lemon juice into a heavy pan and stir over low heat until the sugar has dissolved. Increase the heat to high and let the sugar syrup bubble for 3 minutes. Let cool completely before adding the Champagne. Pour the mixture into a shallow plastic container and freeze for 2 to 3 hours until partially frozen. Scrape the semifrozen granita with a fork and stir up the ice crystals. Return to the freezer until ready to use.

To make the panna cotta,
put the cream, milk, and sugar into a heavy pan over low heat to melt the sugar, stirring occasionally. Meanwhile, soak the gelatin sheets in a shallow dish of cold water for a few minutes.

When the cream
begins to bubble up the sides of the pan, take the pan off the heat. Stir in the white chocolate and continue to stir until it has melted. Squeeze the excess water from the gelatin leaves, add them to the warm mixture, and stir well to dissolve. Pour the mixture into 6–8 darioles or other individual molds. Stand the molds on a tray and refrigerate for 5 to 6 hours or overnight until set. The panna cotta should still have a slight wobble when it is ready.

To turn out,
dip the base of each dariole mold in a bowl of hot water for two seconds, then invert onto a small plate and give the mold a shake to release the panna cotta. Serve each panna cotta surrounded by raspberries and shavings of Champagne granita. Top with a curl of lemon zest if you like.

24 Paella for a crowd

This colorful menu captures some of the best Mediterranean flavors—slow-roasted plum tomatoes, fragrant basil and thyme, freshly marinated anchovies, and a tempti... array of shellfish in the paella. For a more indulgent dessert, serve Coffee & chocola... mousse cups (see page 147) to finish. This menu serves 8–10.

Roasted tomato salad with anchovies & shrimp

Paella

Poached apricots with vanilla crème anglaise

planning your menu

THE DAY BEFORE...
• Prepare the poached apricots for the dessert and leave immersed in the syrup in the refrigerator overnight.
• Make the crème anglaise, cover the surface with plastic wrap to prevent a skin forming and chill.
• Prepare the slow-roasted tomatoes for the salad.

AN HOUR AHEAD...
• Clean the shellfish and prepare the squid for the paella; keep chilled.

HALF AN HOUR AHEAD...
• For the appetizer, cook the shrimp and prepare the other ingredients ready to assemble.
• Prepare all the ingredients for the paella, ready to cook.
• Cook the paella.

JUST BEFORE SERVING...
• Assemble the appetizer and serve.
• Let the paella stand, covered, while you eat the appetizer.
• Serve the paella straight from the pan.
• Plate the dessert and serve.

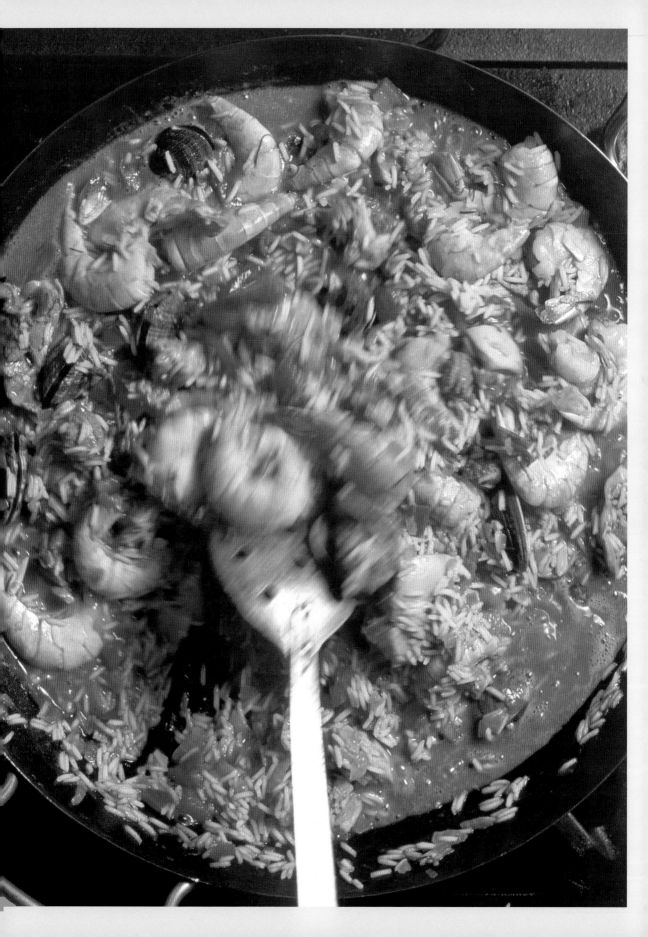

ROASTED TOMATO SALAD WITH ANCHOVIES & SHRIMP

" This gorgeous salad is full of punchy flavors. An ideal appetizer before paella, it also ...kes the perfect starter for an *alfresco* meal, or you can serve it as a side dish for a ...mmer barbecue. Slow-roasting is an excellent way to bring out the flavor of tomatoes. ...recommend you make double the quantity and save the extra for other dishes. Store the ...atoes in clean jars, covered with olive oil, in the refrigerator for up to 3 days. "

] servings

W-ROASTED TOMATOES:
...ium tomatoes
... oil, to drizzle
... thyme sprigs, leaves only
...lic cloves, peeled and thinly sliced
... salt and freshly ground black pepper

...D:
...4oz (300–400g) jumbo shrimp,
...elled and deveined
...ad of lollo rosso (or red oak lettuce),
...mmed
...e bunch of basil, leaves only
... tbsp Classic vinaigrette (see page
...)
...(100g) marinated anchovies (see tip)

IP Freshly marinated anchovies are now ...able from the chilled delicatessen cabinet of ...ted supermarkets. Perfect for salads, they are ...stringent than the salted and oiled options, ... are better suited to cooked dishes.

For the tomatoes, heat the oven to its lowest setting, probably 230°F (100°C). Cut the tomatoes in half lengthwise. Drizzle a little olive oil over the bottom of a large shallow, ovenproof dish and scatter over the thyme leaves, garlic, and a little salt and pepper. Arrange the tomatoes, cut side up, in a single layer over the thyme and garlic. Slowly roast in the oven for about an hour until the tomatoes are soft but still holding their shape. Let cool completely.

For the salad, bring a pan of salted water to a boil and reduce the heat to a simmer. Add the shrimp and cook for 1 to 1½ minutes until they turn opaque. Refresh under cold running water and drain well.

Put the tomatoes into a large bowl. Tear the lettuce and basil leaves into pieces and add them to the bowl with the shrimp. Toss the ingredients with the vinaigrette, then divide among serving plates. Garnish with the marinated anchovies and sprinkle with a little sea salt and black pepper to serve.

PAELLA

To me, paella is the ultimate meal for an informal gathering of friends and family. Indeed, the Spanish have it as part of their Sunday lunch or supper. There are hundreds of variations available, with the common denomination being rice, saffron, and olive oil. This highly flavored version has a bit of everything, but you could pare it down and substitute a few ingredients if you like. 99

8–10 servings

2 skinless and boneless chicken thighs, about 14oz (400g)

4 tbsp olive oil, plus extra to drizzle

1 large Spanish onion, peeled and chopped

1 large red bell pepper, seeded and chopped

3–4 garlic cloves, peeled and thinly sliced

2 long red chiles, sliced on the diagonal

few thyme sprigs

sea salt and freshly ground black pepper

7oz (200g) chorizo sausage, sliced

1 tsp paprika

1lb 2oz (500g) paella rice (or long-grain rice)

splash of dry sherry

½ tsp saffron strands

4 large tomatoes, roughly chopped

1lb 2oz (500g) fresh clams, cleaned (see page 59)

10oz (300g) raw king shrimp (whole or heads removed)

10oz (300g) squid, cleaned and sliced into thin rings

4 cups (400g) peas (thawed, if frozen)

Put the kettle on to boil. Cut the chicken into bite-size pieces. Heat a splash of olive oil in a large paella pan. Add the onion, red bell pepper, garlic, chiles, and thyme, and sauté over high heat for a few minutes until the vegetables start to soften. Season the chicken with salt and pepper, then add to the pan along with the chorizo and paprika. Cook, stirring frequently, over high heat to lightly seal the meat.

Tip in the rice and stir for 2 to 3 minutes, then add a good splash of sherry and pour in enough boiling water to cover the rice by about ½ inch (1cm). Bring to a simmer and sprinkle in the saffron strands, stirring well to distribute them. Add the tomatoes and season well with salt and pepper. Allow to simmer, stirring frequently, for about 10 to 12 minutes.

Add the clams and shrimp, with a little more boiling water if needed, and stir through. Cook over medium heat for 3 minutes until the shrimp are opaque and the clams start to open up. Finally, stir in the squid and peas. The squid should only take 1 to 2 minutes to cook—it will turn opaque when it is ready. Taste and adjust the seasoning.

Take the pan off the heat, cover with foil, and let stand for 5 minutes to allow the flavors to meld together. Drizzle a little olive oil over the paella and bring the pan to the table to serve.

POACHED APRICOTS
WITH VANILLA CREME ANGLAISE

" Ripe fresh apricots are poached in a sugar syrup infused with aromatics to bring out their flavor. You can poach the fruit a day ahead and keep it in the refrigerator. Save the leftover syrup in a jar, ready to drizzle over ice cream or fruit salads. "

8–10 servings

3 cups (750ml) Sugar syrup
(see page 248)
vanilla bean
cinnamon stick
lemon grass stalk, split lengthwise
tsp coriander seeds
tsp black peppercorns
16–20 just ripe fresh apricots
quantity Crème anglaise (see
page 248)

Pour the sugar syrup into a shallow, wide pan. Split the vanilla bean and scrape out the seeds with the back of a knife, adding them to the pan along with the vanilla bean, cinnamon, lemon grass, coriander seeds, and peppercorns. Bring to a simmer.

Add half the apricots and poach for about 10 to 15 minutes until tender but not oversoft, carefully turning several times during cooking. Remove with a slotted spoon to a large plate. Add the rest of the apricots to the sugar syrup and poach in the same way, then transfer to the plate and leave until cool enough to handle.

Strain the syrup through a strainer into a large bowl. Peel off the skins from the apricots, then cut in half and discard the pits. Immerse the apricots in the sugar syrup, cover the bowl with plastic wrap, and chill for at least 3 hours or overnight.

Arrange the apricots on wide plates and drizzle with a little of their aromatic syrup. Pour the crème anglaise around the fruit and serve.

25 Summer entertaining

A sumptuous summer spread centered around a freshly baked salmon with gorgeous accompaniments. I start the meal with a selection of interesting little appetizers and finish with hot soufflés that taste as amazing as they look. This menu serves 6–8.

Antipasti:
+ Stuffed zucchini rolls   + Balsamic beet with Roquefort

+ Prosciutto, sage & Parmesan puffs   + Marinated mushrooms

Salmon baked with herbs & caramelized lemons
+ Pink grapefruit hollandaise

+ Romaine, red onion & asparagus salad   + Minted new potatoes (see page 191)

Passion fruit & banana soufflé

planning your menu

A FEW DAYS AHEAD...
• Order the whole salmon from your fish supplier (arranging to collect it a day ahead, or on the day if possible).

SEVERAL HOURS IN ADVANCE...
• For the antipasti, prepare the marinated mushrooms and balsamic beet; keep both chilled.

TWO HOURS AHEAD...
• Make the crème pâtissière base for the soufflé; let cool. Prepare the soufflé dishes.
• Scrub the potatoes and immerse in cold water.
• Make the choux paste for the puffs; let cool.

AN HOUR OR SO AHEAD...
• Prepare the zucchini strips and filling ready to assemble; chill.
• Prepare the salad, ready to assemble.
• Add the fruit purée and passion fruit juice to the soufflé base.
• Make and bake the Parmesan puffs (or do so earlier and keep warm).
• Prepare the salmon ready for baking.
• Prepare the hollandaise; keep warm.
• Assemble the zucchini rolls.

JUST BEFORE SERVING...
• Assemble the antipasti and serve.
• Bake the salmon and cook the potatoes while you eat the appetizer.
• Let the salmon rest while you dress the potatoes and assemble the salad. Serve the main course.
• Finish the soufflés, bake, and serve immediately.

234

ANTIPASTI

I love the way Italians start a meal with a platter of tempting foods to tantalize the palate. This is my take on antipasti—a selection of interesting warm and cold bites that c be prepared in advance.

Stuffed zucchini rolls

6–8 servings

4 small zucchini, trimmed
olive oil, to oil and drizzle
1 cup (250g) ricotta
juice of ½ lemon
splash of extra virgin olive oil
sea salt and freshly ground black
  pepper
handful of basil leaves, chopped
⅓ cup (50g) pine nuts, toasted
balsamic vinegar, to drizzle

Slice the zucchini lengthwise, using a
swivel vegetable peeler or a mandolin and select about 40 good strips. Place th
zucchini strips on an oiled tray and brush with olive oil. Season with salt and
pepper and chill for 20 minutes.

Mix the ricotta with the lemon juice, extra virgin olive oil, a
seasoning to taste, then fold in the chopped basil and pine nuts. Place a small
teaspoonful of ricotta mixture on one end of a zucchini strip and roll up. Repeat
use up all the filling. Arrange the zucchini cannelloni on a plate and grind over
some black pepper. Drizzle with a little olive oil and balsamic vinegar and serve

Balsamic beet with Roquefort

6–8 servings

1⅓lb (600g) cooked baby beet, peeled
3–4 tbsp olive oil
6–7 tbsp balsamic vinegar
sea salt and freshly ground black pepper
5oz (150g) Roquefort
1–2 tsp sesame seeds, toasted

Halve the beet or quarter, depending on size. Heat
olive oil in a large sauté pan, add the beet, and sauté for 2 to 3 minutes
Add the balsamic vinegar and season with salt and pepper. Toss to coa
the beet in the syrupy glaze. Transfer to a bowl, let cool completely, the
chill for a few hours.

Crumble the Roquefort over the beet
and sprinkle with toasted sesame seeds to serve.

rosciutto, sage & Parmesan puffs

eat the oven to 400°F (200°C). Put the butter and scant (220ml) water into a heavy pan. Heat slowly to melt the butter, then turn e heat and bring to a rolling boil. Meanwhile, sift the flour and salt ther. As soon as the liquid comes up to a boil, tip in all the flour and salt take the pan off the heat. Beat vigorously with a wooden spoon until the re comes together as a paste and leaves the sides of the pan. Spread plate and let cool.

eturn the paste to the pan (or place in a bowl) and in the eggs, a little at a time, until soft, shiny, and smooth. The mixture ld have a dropping consistency (you may not need all of the egg). Beat in hopped prosciutto, sage, and Parmesan until evenly incorporated. Lightly se a large baking sheet. Spoon the mixture into a pastry bag fitted with a ch (1–1.5-cm) plain tip and pipe into small 1¼–1½-inch (3–4-cm) circles e baking sheet, spacing them about 2 inches (5cm) apart to leave room xpansion. Bake for 20 to 25 minutes or until the pastries are well risen golden brown. Serve immediately or keep warm in a low oven.

Makes about 35
6½ tbsp (85g) unsalted butter, plus extra to grease
¾ cup (100g) all-purpose flour
pinch of salt
3 medium eggs, beaten
4oz (100g) prosciutto, minced
4–5 sage leaves, finely shredded
1½oz (40g) Parmesan, finely grated

larinated mushrooms

eat the olive oil in a large wide heavy pan. n it is almost smoking, add the mushrooms and sauté over high for about 5 minutes until they are lightly golden. Tip in the shallots season well with salt and pepper. Sauté until the shallots have ened. Add a splash of wine vinegar and let the liquid bubble for a minutes. Drizzle generously with olive oil and allow to cool to room perature. Sprinkle with tarragon to serve.

6–8 servings
4–5 tbsp olive oil, plus extra to drizzle
1lb 2oz (500g) white mushrooms, cleaned, trimmed, and halved if large
2–3 shallots, peeled and sliced
sea salt and freshly ground black pepper
generous splash of white wine vinegar
small bunch of tarragon, leaves only

SALMON BAKED WITH HERBS & CARAMELIZED LEMONS

66 The delicate flavor of salmon really comes through when it is oven-steamed on a bed of herbs. The juice of the caramelized lemons further enhances the fish. You can serve the salmon simply with its cooking juices or elevate the dish to another level by serving it with a gorgeous Pink grapefruit hollandaise (see page 243). 99

6–8 servings

1 whole salmon, about 3½lb (1.6kg),
   scaled, cleaned, and washed
olive oil, for cooking and to drizzle
sea salt and freshly ground black pepper
2 bay leaves
few sprigs each of rosemary, thyme, basil,
   sage, and parsley
1 head of garlic (unpeeled), halved
   horizontally, then broken into cloves
2–3 lemon grass stalks, split in half
   lengthwise and bruised with the back
   of a knife
1 large or 3 small lemons, thickly sliced
5–6 star anise
1 tsp mixed (or black) peppercorns

Trim a little off the tail and fins of the salmon with kitchen scissors and pat dry with paper towels. Pat the cavity dry. Score the skin of the salmon on both sides, at ½–¾ inch (1–2cm) intervals. Rub all over with olive oil, salt, and pepper.

Tear two sheets of foil, large enough to envelope the salmon easily. Lay one on top of the other on the counter and scatter the bay leaves, herb sprigs, garlic, and lemon grass over the middle of the foil. Lay the fish on the bed of herbs and tuck some of the flavorings into the cavity.

Sauté the lemon slices in a little olive oil for 2 to 3 minutes until caramelized around the edges, seasoning them with salt and pepper. Let cool slightly. Tuck the caramelized lemon slices around the fish, placing some in the cavity and some on top. Scatter the star anise and peppercorns over and around the fish, putting some inside the cavity. Drizzle the salmon with a little olive oil. Heat the oven to 375°F (190°C).

Fold the edges of the foil tightly together over the salmon to seal, leaving some space in the package for steam to surround and cook the fish. Put the salmon package in the roasting pan and cook in the center of the oven for 25 to 30 minutes, depending on the thickness of the salmon. Remove from the oven and without unwrapping the foil package, rest the fish for 5 to 10 minutes.

Unwrap the salmon and peel off the skin with a spatula. Use the back of a spoon to slide the fish off the bone. Serve individual portions garnished with the caramelized lemons and accompanied by the pink grapefruit hollandaise and salad.

Pink grapefruit hollandaise

Put the egg yolks, grapefruit zest and juice, coriander, and 1 tbsp warm water into a heatproof bowl and set over a pan of simmering water. Whisk, using a balloon whisk, until the mixture is pale, creamy, and falls in a slow ribbon. Remove the bowl from the heat and whisk for another 3 minutes until the mixture has cooled slightly. Whisk in 1 tbsp olive oil, then gradually whisk in the rest in a thin steady stream until it is all incorporated and the sauce is a good coating consistency. Season with salt and pepper to taste and add a little extra grapefruit juice if you think it needs it. If the sauce is a little too thick, stir in a tiny splash of warm water. Keep warm in a bain-marie (or bowl over hot water) until ready to serve.

Makes about 300ml

3 egg yolks
finely grated zest of 1 pink grapefruit
juice of ½ pink grapefruit, plus an extra squeeze to taste
6–8 coriander seeds, finely crushed
⅔ cup (150ml) light olive oil
sea salt and freshly ground white pepper

Romaine, red onion & asparagus salad

–8 servings
Ooz (300g) asparagus spears, trimmed and stalks peeled
ea salt and freshly ground black pepper
large romaine lettuce, washed
red onion, peeled and thinly sliced
–4 tbsp Classic vinaigrette (see page 247)

Blanch the asparagus in a pan of boiling salted water for 1½ to 2 minutes until just tender. Drain and refresh under cold running water. Trim off the base of the lettuces and arrange the leaves over a large serving bowl. Put a blanched asparagus spear into the center of each lettuce leaf and scatter over the sliced onion. Sprinkle with salt and pepper and drizzle with a little vinaigrette just before serving.

PASSION FRUIT & BANANA SOUFFLÉ

" This is a soufflé that Angela Hartnett serves at the Connaught and it is amazingly good. The banana and passion fruit marry perfectly, giving the soufflé an extraordinary, delicate, and subtle flavor. "

Makes 6–8

CRÈME PATISSIÈRE BASE:
⅔ cup (150ml) milk
½ cup (100ml) heavy cream
1 tbsp (15g) all-purpose flour
2 tsp (10g) cornstarch
4 large egg yolks
¼ cup (50g) superfine sugar

SOUFFLÉ:
4 ripe passion fruit
1 banana, about 4oz (100g), peeled
squeeze of lemon juice
1 tbsp banana liqueur (optional)
about 1½ tbsp (20g) butter, melted, to brush
¼ cup (50g) superfine sugar, plus extra to dust
grated chocolate, to dust (optional)
4 large egg whites
confectioners' sugar, to dust

TIP Don't be tempted to open the oven door until the soufflés are almost ready or they may collapse.

For the crème patissière
base, heat the milk and cream in a heavy pan until almost boiling. Sift the flour and cornstarch together. Beat the egg yolks and sugar together in a large bowl, then mix in the flour. Add a splash of the hot creamy milk and whisk well until the mixture is smooth, then gradually whisk in the rest of the milk. Pour back into the pan and whisk over medium-low heat for 3 to 5 minutes until thickened and smooth. Transfer to a bowl, cover, and cool to room temperature, stirring occasionally to prevent a skin forming.

Halve the passion fruit
and scoop out the seeds and juice into a strainer set over a bowl. Press to extract the juice, then pour into a blender. Break the banana into pieces and add to the blender with the lemon juice and liqueur if using. Whiz until smooth, then stir this mixture into the crème patissière and set aside.

Heat the oven
to 375°F (190°C). Brush 6–8 deep ramekins with a generous layer of melted butter, using upward strokes. Dust the insides either with superfine sugar or grated chocolate (or coat some with each) and chill to set.

When ready to serve,
whisk the egg whites in a clean bowl to firm peaks, then gradually whisk in the ¼ cup (50g) superfine sugar a spoonful at a time to make a firm, glossy meringue. Whisk a third of the meringue into the crème patissière base, then very carefully fold in the rest, using a large metal spoon.

Divide the soufflé mix
among the prepared dishes and tap them on the counter to level the mixture. Smooth the tops with a spatula, then run the spatula around the edge. (This helps the soufflés to rise evenly.) Sit the ramekins on a wide baking tray and bake for 10 to 12 minutes until well risen and lightly golden on top. The soufflés should wobble gently in the middle when ready. Dust with confectioners' sugar and serve at once.

BASICS

Chicken stock

Put 1 chopped carrot, 1 chopped onion, 2 sliced celery stalks, and 1 sliced leek in large pan with 2 tbsp olive oil and cook over medium heat until golden. Add a sprig thyme, 1 bay leaf, 3 peeled garlic cloves, 2 tbsp tomato paste, and 2 tbsp all-purpose flour and cook, stirring, for a few minutes. Add 2¼lb (1kg) raw chicken bones, cover with plenty of cold water, and season lightly. Bring to a boil and skim. Simmer for 1 hour and then pass through a chinois or fine strainer. Adjust the seasoning.

Brown chicken stock
This is used for a greater depth of flavor. For the above recipe, roasting the chicken bones at 400°F (200°C) for 20 minutes before adding them. Brown duck stock can be made in the same way.

Fish stock

This is quick to make, using fish trimmings, or you can use crab or lobster shells. Heat 2 tbsp olive oil in a large pan. Add ½ chopped onion, ½ sliced celery stalk, and 1 chopped fennel slice, and cook until soft but not colored. Add 2¼lb (1kg) fish trimmings (white fish bones and heads), a glass of white wine, and enough water cover. Bring to a boil, season lightly, and simmer for 20 minutes. Pass through a chinois or fine strainer and adjust the seasoning.

TIP Make up these stocks in batches and keep them in the refrigerator (for up to 5 days) or freezer (up to 3 months) until required.

A poaching liquor used for cooking whole fish and shellfish, such as lobster and crab. Place 1 chopped carrot, 1 chopped onion, a few bay leaves, 1 tsp black peppercorns, 1 tsp rock salt, and ⅓ cup (100ml) white wine vinegar in a large pan and pour in 3⅓ cups (800ml) water. Bring to a boil, then let simmer for 20 to 30 minutes. Strain through a fine strainer and use immediately or cool and keep in the refrigerator for up to 3 days.

eloute
es about 2 cups (500ml)

Heat a piece of butter in a wide pan. Stir in 3 minced shallots and sauté gently for about 10 minutes until soft but not colored. Pour in ¾ cup (200ml) dry white wine and ¾ cup (200ml) dry vermouth and boil until reduced by half. Then add 1¾ cups (400ml) stock (fish, vegetable, or chicken), return to a boil and reduce by half. Stir in 1¼ cups (300ml) heavy cream and simmer gently until the sauce is the consistency of pouring cream. Season to taste with salt and pepper and strain the sauce through a fine strainer.

lassic vinaigrette
es about 1 cup (250ml)

Put ⅓ cup (100ml) extra virgin olive oil, ⅓ cup (100ml) peanut oil, 1 scant tsp Dijon mustard, 1 tbsp lemon juice, 2 tbsp white wine vinegar, and some sea salt and pepper in a measuring cup and whisk together until emulsified. Pour into a clean bottle, seal, and refrigerate. Shake well before using.

ayonnaise
es about 1½ cups (300ml)

In a mixing bowl, whisk together 2 large egg yolks, 1 tsp white wine vinegar, 1 tsp English mustard, and a pinch of sea salt. Slowly add 1¼ cups (300ml) peanut oil, drop by drop to begin with, then in a thin stream, whisking constantly until thick and emulsified. (If the mayonnaise splits, mix another egg yolk with a pinch of seasoning and a little mustard and slowly whisk in the split mixture. It should re-emulsify). Season with salt and pepper to taste and chill. Use within 3 days.

Crème anglaise
Makes about 5 cups (1.2 liters)

Heat 2 cups (500ml) whole milk, 2 cups (500ml) heavy cream, and 1 tbsp sugar in heavy pan. Scrape the seeds from 2 split vanilla beans and add to the pan. In a la bowl, beat together 12 egg yolks and ⅓ cup (85g) superfine sugar. As soon as the milk and cream begin to boil, take the pan off the heat. Gradually pour the hot liqui onto the sugary yolks, whisking continuously. Strain the mixture through a strainer a clean pan. Stir the mixture over low heat until the custard thickens enough to thir coat the back of a spoon. Remove the pan from the heat and strain the custard ag through a fine strainer. Let cool, stirring occasionally to prevent a skin forming.

Sugar syrup
Makes about 3 cups (750ml)

Put 1¼ cups (250g) superfine sugar, 2 cups (500ml) water, and the finely pared ze of ½ lemon into a heavy pan. Bring slowly to a boil, stirring to help dissolve the sug Bring the syrup to a boil and let it bubble for 5 minutes. Cool completely then trans to a sealed container and refrigerate, unless using immediately.

French meringue nests
Makes about 8–10

These are the perfect base for serving soft fruits with whipped cream or ice cream. Heat the oven to the lowest setting, 230°F (100°C). Using a hand-held electric bea whisk 2 large egg whites in a clean, grease-free bowl with a pinch of salt until the e whites hold firm peaks. Gradually whisk in ½ cup (100g) superfine sugar, 1 tbsp at time. Continue to whisk until the meringue is glossy and holds its shape. Spoon or pipe the meringue into round disks, about ¾ inch (2cm) thick, on a lined baking tra Bake for at least 2 hours until slightly crusty on top, then turn off the heat and let th meringues dry out in the oven for 6 hours or overnight. Peel the meringues off the baking parchment and store in an airtight container for up to a week.

Sift 1⅔ cups (225g) all-purpose flour and 1 tsp salt into a food processor. Add ⅔ cup (140g) cold unsalted butter, in small pieces, and whiz for 10 seconds until the mixture resembles coarse bread crumbs, then tip into a mixing bowl. Pour in 4 tbsp of ice cold water and stir the mixture with a knife until the dough comes together. Add another 1 tbsp water if it seems too dry. (Don't make it too wet, as a crumbly dough results in a lighter crust.) Press the mixture into a dough, wrap in plastic wrap, and chill for at least 30 minutes before using.

Put 9 tbsp (125g) unsalted butter (at room temperature) and scant ½ cup (90g) superfine sugar in a food processor and whiz until just combined. Add a large egg and whiz for 30 seconds. Tip in 1¾ cups (250g) all-purpose flour and process for a few seconds until the dough just comes together. (Be careful not to overprocess or the dough will become tough.) Add 1 tbsp cold water if the dough seems too dry. Knead lightly on a floured counter, then shape into a flat disk, wrap in plastic wrap, and chill for 30 minutes before rolling out.

Sift ¾ cup (100g) all-purpose flour and ¼ tsp fine sea salt into a large bowl and make a well in the center. Beat 1 large egg and ¾ cup (200ml) milk together and pour into the well. Gradually whisk the flour into the wet mixture until the batter is well combined and smooth. Let the batter stand for 20 minutes. Heat a nonstick crêpe pan with a piece of butter. Give the batter a stir and pour a small ladleful into the pan. Quickly swirl the batter around the pan, pouring off any excess, and cook until golden brown at the edges. Flip the crêpe to cook the other side for 30 seconds. Repeat until all the batter has been used.

Herb crêpes   Add 2 tbsp of chopped mixed herbs, such as parsley, tarragon, chervil, and chives, to the egg and milk mixture, then whisk into the flour. Continue as for basic crêpes.

INDEX

ACKNOWLEDGMENTS

A book of this quality can only be put together with the strength and dedication of the talented team that I am so luck to be working with. Once again, I am indebted to my "adopted son," Mark Sargeant, who has worked tirelessly on ever photo shoot and always manages to lighten the day with his humor. Mark now leaves the family to get married, but remains my right-hand man. I am very grateful to Pat Llewellyn and everyone at Optomen TV for helping me. Pat and I work together almost like tomato and basil in the kitchen. And I owe a special thanks to my dear Emily, for her hard w patience, and understanding of what precious time I have. Dynamic meetings with her left me enough time to play foo ... brilliant, Emily.

A big thank you to Helen Lewis, as always. Helen helped me with my first ever book, so she has been there from start and knows me inside out, which is apparent throughout this book. I now regard her as an integral member of ou kitchen brigade. And to the newly found yummy mummy of the photography world, Jill, who is terrific. Her enthusiasm infectious, though I cringe when she calls me poppet! And Janet Illsley, for being forever demanding and scrutinizing editorial-wise, a job well done yet again...I think I owe you twelve dinners now, twelve tables for two. And, of course, An Furniss and Alison Cathie, for trusting the vision to get behind this campaign.

And thanks to everyone at Gordon Ramsay Holdings, from Gillian Thomson to Chris Hutcheson. Also to Jo Barne her strategy and determination to make this book a big hit. And to Tony Turnbull from The Times who has shared my passion. Without all these people listed, this book wouldn't f...... be here!

And finally to my four new sous chefs Jack, Holly, Megan, and Matilda. A huge thanks for tasting all the recipes your father is cooking ... and under no circumstances do you send any of his food back. Thanks, also, to my mother, He for being a great prop... you may not like having your picture taken Mom, but you look terrific! And last but not least, tc most patient woman in Britain today, my beloved wife Tana.

Editorial director **Anne Furniss**
Art director **Helen Lewis**
Project editor **Janet Illsley**
Editor **Kathy Steer**
Photographer **Jill Mead**
Food stylist **Mark Sargeant**
Home economist **Emily Quah**
Assistant designer **Katherine Case**
Editorial assistant **Andrew Bayliss**
Production **Vincent Smith, Ruth Deary**

Optomen Television Production Consultants:

Patricia Llewellyn (Managing director); Eileen Herlihy (Series producer); Sarah Wood (Producer); Sarah Durdin-Robertson (Assistant producer, food)

All survey statistics used in this book are derived from the F Word/Gfk NOP Survey, February 2006.

Optomen Television Limited
1, Valentine Place
London SE1 8QH
www.optomen.com

First published in 2006 by
Quadrille Publishing Limited
Alhambra House,
27-31 Charing Cross Road,
London WC2H 0LS
www.quadrille.co.uk

This book is also published in the USA
as a hardback edition with the title
Gordon Ramsay's Sunday Lunch

Text © 2006 Gordon Ramsay
Photography © 2006 Jill Mead
Design and layout © 2006 Quadrille
Publishing Limited
Format and programme © 2006 Optomen
Television Limited

Library and Archives Canada Catalog in Publication
Ramsay, Gordon
        Gordon Ramsay's family fa

ISBN 978-1-55470-222-0

        1. Cookery. 2. Menus.
I. Title. II. Title: Family fare.

TX714.R3525 2010   641.5
C2009-905884-7

ONTARIO ARTS COUN
CONSEIL DES ARTS DE

The publisher gratefully acknowledges support of the Canada Council for the and the Ontario Arts Council for its pu program. We acknowledge the suppo Government of Ontario through the O Media Development Corporation's On Book Initiative.

We acknowledge the financial suppor Government of Canada through the B Publishing Industry Development Pro (BPIDP) for our publishing activities.

Key Porter Books Limited
Six Adelaide Street East, Tenth Floor
Toronto, Ontario
Canada M5C 1H6
www.keyporter.com

Printed and bound in China
10 11 12 13 14 5 4 3 2 1

optomen